INVEST

With As Little As $100

A guide to investing in financial instruments

By Roger Neal Smith

Dedication

This book is dedicated to Roger B. and Georgia Smith, Donna Taylor, Denise Caldwell, and Kay Black – my father, mother, and three sisters. It is also dedicated to KS, RS and LT – the other people who are important in my life, but whose identities must remain secret because, I believe, they came to Earth from other planets that exploded when they were very young, and want to live their lives amongst us on Earth undetected. However, if none of the people listed want to admit knowing me, then never mind.

Table of Contents

Preface iii

Chapter 1 -- The Creation 1
  Introduction 1
  Investments Illustrated 6
  An Amazing Girl Named Grace 9

Chapter 2 -- Low Risk Investments 11
  Bank Instruments 11
    Savings Accounts 12
    Certificates of Deposit 15
  U.S. Government Instruments 19
    Treasury Bills 20
    Treasury Notes 22
    Treasury Bonds 24
  Money Market Funds 26
  Municipal Bonds 28
  Brokerage Instruments 33
  Credit Union Accounts 35

Chapter 3 -- Moderate Risk Investments 39
  Investment Stocks 39
  Corporate Bonds 47
  Preferred Stock 52
  Commercial Paper 54
  Mutual Funds 57
  Unit Investment Trusts 68

Chapter 4 -- High Risk Investments 71
  Speculative Stocks 72
  Commodities 75
  Stock Options 85
  Foreign Currency 93
  Limited Partnerships 99

TABLE OF CONTENTS

Chapter 5 -- Brokers 103

Chapter 6 -- Conclusion...109

Appendix A -- Invest or Not Invest......................................115

Appendix B -- Bond Pricing Explored 121

Appendix C -- Present Value Tables 131

Appendix D -- Present Value of an Annuity 137

Appendix E -- Synthetic Bonds...143

Appendix F -- Talk Finance 147

Appendix G -- Directory of Publications 173

Acknowledgments

In most books, this is the section where the author thanks everyone from his wife, for giving the support and encouragement needed to complete the book, to his obstetrician for not making a major mistake during his birth. However, being of questionable mind and body, I decided to do it differently. Rather than bore you with an endless list of people who have inspired, counseled and humored me, I elected to mention most of the people inside the book.

The names of many of the people who have been directly or indirectly responsible for this literary masterpiece being completed are used in my examples. I used some people's first names, and other's last names. Neither the number of times, sequence of use nor whether the first or last name was used has any bearing on their degree of input or inspiration (only my hairdresser and I know for sure).

Since my memory is as long as a chicken's lips, it is quite possible that I have overlooked someone. To those I have neglected to mention, I wish to say: 1) I'm terribly sorry, and 2) give me a call (the number's listed) and I will mention you in the next edition.

NOTICE

To the best of the author's knowledge, the information contained in this book is accurate. However, do to the volatile nature of finance and the facts that securities laws and regulations change over time and interest rates fluctuate on a continual basis, the author assumes no responsibility or liability for errors or any consequences arising from the use of the information contained herein. Final determination of the suitability of any investment contemplated by the reader and the manner in which such investment will be used is the sole responsibility of the user.

(In other words when I wrote this book, I believed that everything was accurate. However, over time, things change. So keep in mind the following: 1) the government is constantly changing the rules and making new laws because thieves are always finding new ways of trying to steal your money; 2) don't come to me saying "… liar, liar" because when I wrote the book I said that interest on an investment was at one rate, and by the time you read the book they were different; and 3) since I have no idea of who you are, how much you have to invest or how much risk you are willing to take, you have to make your own investment decisions – I can't make them for you.)

Preface

Why I Wrote This Book

I never intended to write a book on investing. I was satisfied with speculating in the commodities and options markets, and investing in the stock market. I learned about these and other financial instruments by reading numerous books on finance, by talking to other investors and while working on a MBA degree at the University of Chicago, an institution noted for excellence in finance.

After consuming mass quantities of technical jargon, I found that all of the books had three major shortcomings. First, most of them assumed that the reader was already a financial wizard. Terms such as leverage and hedging were not explained so that Freddie and Mary Kruger could feel comfortable using them. I liken the mystique used in the area of finance with the same kind utilized in law. Just as a lawyer justifies his existence and big fees by using terms that humans don't understand, bankers and brokers also use words that help keep their positions secure. This is not to say that people in these professions have no other function than to use big words and take your money. On the contrary. Both brokers and bankers keep a constant vigil on what's happening in the wonderful world of finance. Most people have neither the time nor the desire to do so.

The second shortcoming was that there are no single books available from which people can learn about many of the investment possibilities open to them (most of the books are married). There are books covering many of the financial instruments individually, but no one book explaining them all. You either have to know exactly what you are interested in or you have to spend a lot of time and money obtaining and piecing together the material -- only to discover that you are still not sure what to do.

Third, most books, except for school texts, are primarily about investment strategy. That is, they discuss things such as how to make a killing in the Options market or how to recognize stocks with the greatest potential. While strategy is a good thing to know, if you don't feel that you have a good understanding of what options or commodities are, all of the strategy in the world will not help.

After considering all of the literary shortcomings, I still had no desire to write a book. I did feel that one what was necessary, but I figured that someone else could write it. I decided to write this book because of my father and people like him. My father, like many others, had an extremely conservative and traditional investment philosophy. I talked to him about the attributes and deficiencies possessed by various investments. Although he agreed with the things I said, he took no action. I feel that the reason for his inaction was in part due to the fact that no reference material was readily available. Having to rely on one's memory, especially when money is involved, can be very difficult. My primary reason for writing this book is to make people realize that investing and saving money is not a difficult thing to do.

Why I Can Write This Book

If you are actually taking time to read this section of the book, either you have nothing better to do or you're probably wondering "... what makes you think you're qualified to write a book like this?" So, instead of having to answer that question constantly, I've decided to answer before it's asked.

I worked as a Financial Consultant with one of the world's largest securities firms. During my tenure there, I accomplished the following:

- Managed more than $150 million of other people's money.
- Served over 600 clients worldwide, which included both businesses and individuals.
- Served as a portfolio manager and retirement planning specialist for numerous businesses and individuals.
- Consulted with private corporations desiring to raise capital or go public, and consulted with public corporations needing assistance in raising funds or increasing the value of their stock prices.
- Personally conducted numerous seminars and classes on investing for both businesses and individuals.
- Have written a variety of articles about investing.

- Have had the opportunity of investing in the majority of the investments discussed in this book.
- Have created a public company from the ground up.
- Have taught business and finance at various colleges and universities in Southern California for over 20 years.

Why You Should Read This Book

Anyone can achieve a level of success if they consider two things. First, do as much financial planning as possible. Whether they know it or not, everyone plans.

Imagine that you want to drive from your home to a movie theatre. Since the world is round, theoretically you can drive in the opposite direction of your destination and still get to see the movie. However, a better way of getting there is to plan your route. If you have never been to the area where the movie theater is located, you will probably ask for directions from someone who has been there or look at a map. Also, since the movie theater is not open twenty-four hours a day, you will plan on a time to leave your home so you will get there before it begins.

Investing should be done in the same manner, but you can do it without a car. Rather than just making arbitrary investment decisions, plan on where you want to be financially and when you want to get to your destination. If you don't know the best route, ask a knowledgeable person for the best directions. Don't fall into the trap of using a friend's plan. Although the person might have the best intentions to help guide you, their needs or tolerance for risk might be very different from yours. *(She could be giving you the best way to go to the movie theater on the east side of town, while you actually want to go to the one on the west side.)* If you are willing to make a plan to spend $20 for a movie, you should be willing to make a plan to invest for your future.

The second thing to realize is that you have access to the same investment tools as everyone else. However, you need to know which tools to use and how to use them. Just as it is impossible to build a solid house with only one type of building tool, you can't build a solid financial base with only one type of investment tool. Therefore, to take some of the mysticism out of investing, to help provide a section of an investing road map and to tell you about the financial tools available to build your financial future, I offer this book.

Chapter 1
-- The Creation

Introduction

In the beginning, God created the heavens, the earth, and the common man and woman. (They were originally called "manomaviticanovich" and "womanomaviticanovich", but were later changed to "man" and "woman" to make it easier to remember and spell.) After the misunderstanding with the apple and the snake, we have had a never ending desire to improve our standard of living by buying trivial things like food, shelter, clothing and an occasional lottery ticket. This frivolous spending has resulted in us having very little money left to save or invest. However, once in a while something goes right and we end up with a few extra dollars after all the bills have been paid.

Once the initial shock of having extra cash subsides, we begin thinking of ways to invest this new-found wealth. After not being able to come up with any great ideas, the money either sits in a checking account where it earns nothing, or it is put into a savings account where it gathers a whopping three percent interest. While the bank is paying us this generous sum, it is making at least two or three times as much by loaning our money to those of us who didn't have any extra.

Although we, the depositors, and the bank both appear to be better off, we are not as well off as one might expect. The reason is because of a little thing called inflation. True, the bank will pay us 3¢ per year for each dollar we save. However, if inflation causes prices to rise by five percent, the item we bought for $1.00 now costs $1.05. Therefore, we are actually 2¢ poorer! Moreover, once the government takes their portion of the 3¢ we earn, we have even less.

In 1999, Masami Inoue had $2.00. With one of her dollars, she purchased a pair of socks. She put the other dollar into a savings account paying 3% interest. One year later, Masami decided that she needed a new pair of socks, so she went to the bank to get her money and close the account. When closing her account, the bank gave her $1.03. Masami was as happy as a cow being milked by a farmer with warm hands because she knew that the new socks will only cost $1.00, which meant that she had an extra 3¢. When Masami got to the store, she became as sad as a three-legged dog in a horse race. She realized that, because inflation had increased by 5%, the price of the new socks went up to $1.05. Since she only had $1.03, she had to go sockless or wear her old pair.

Granted, having our money in the bank making three cents per dollar is far better than keeping it in an old sock making nothing *(especially if the sock emits noxious fumes every time you are within five feet of it).* However, there are ways in which we can actually come out on top. Some of those ways are discussed in the following chapters.

After talking to many people, I found that most believed they needed thousands of dollars to invest in financial instruments, except for savings accounts. I also discovered that many people would like to invest their money in financial instruments other than those offered by banks, but they either did not know what other types of investments are available or were unable to find information written for humans to read.

This book, which is also known as "Clarence", has been written to help you to better understand the "what" and "how" of investing in financial instruments. By reading it, you will learn about many of the various investment opportunities that exist. Think of Clarence as a reference source. Take it with you wherever you go. Refer to Clarence when talking to friends, neighbors and relatives you like. Take it to dinner and a movie occasionally *(it likes science fiction, romantic comedies, Jazz [Hubert Laws, not Kenny G] and Sushi).*

By discussing the available options, Clarence has been written to illustrate various ways in which you might be able to make more money. It will take the mystery out of words like "Stock Option;" "Treasury Bill" and "Commercial Paper," and will cover many areas of investing -- from the very safe to the very risky. It will also show you what to look for in an investment and will suggest when to invest.

Clarence was not written to show you how to make a million dollars in the stock market, how to be an arbitrager in the foreign exchange market or how to be a better shopper in the supermarket. To do so would require a book several times larger, with a lot of technical terms and explanations that would defeat my purpose. Also, there is no need to go into great detail since there are already many good (and bad) publications available covering most of the topics. A directory of publications has been included in Appendix G. It lists other publications that cover financial investments in more detail and is indexed by subject matter for easy reference.

Investments span a wide gap - from the very safe, to the very risky. Entering into safer ones is called "investing" because people normally do so with the feeling that they will make a reasonable profit and their money is relatively safe. Entering into riskier ones is what I refer to as "speculating" because by doing so, people are taking greater chances in the hope of making greater profits. Consider the following example:

Jim Hankins and Ron Turner, two enterprising individuals, both received $100 from their fathers. Ron decides to put his money into an account that guarantees to pay him 5% interest per year for the next five years. At the end of the fifth year, Ron will have $125.

Ron has chosen an instrument in which he is confident that he will not lose his original investment, and is sure that he will make $25. Although Ron will not make a lot of money by investing this way, he will be $25 richer in five years.

With his $100, Jim decides to take a chance by opening a lemonade stand. He spends $40 for lemons and sugar, $20 for paper cups and $40 for cookies to sell. Jim feels that since the temperature outside is ninety degrees, if he opens the stand on the beach he will make a lot more money than if he opens it in front of his house. Jim also feels that if he sells all of the lemonade and cookies he will make $125. His $25 profit, *however, is made in one day, which results in an annual rate of return of ninety percent.*

Jim has chosen a risky (speculative) method of investing. In less than one day, he can make a 25% profit on his investment. However, because he is taking a chance, there is also a possibility of losing his total investment. If it starts to rain, everyone will leave the beach and he will not sell any lemonade or cookies. Even if it doesn't rain, there is no guarantee that people will want to buy anything from him or that he will make as much as he expects.

The previous examples demonstrates the difference between risky and safe investments. Ron decided to put money into an account with a guaranteed return and wait five years to make his $25 profit. Jim, on the other hand, decided to speculate and chose a much quicker, riskier method of trying to increase his wealth.

The word "investing" can be defined as "... *putting money into stocks, bonds, businesses, real estate, etc., for the purpose of obtaining an income or profit at some future time.*" That "future time" could be one hour fifty-seven minutes, fifty-two years, or one thousand years. Any time after right "now" qualifies as a future time.

This book's primary function is to discuss the various financial instruments available to you. That is, stocks, bonds, treasury bills, etc. However, prior to beginning, I feel that an honorable mention should also be given to some of the non-financial instruments in which you can invest. One of the biggest differences between financial and non-financial instruments is that you usually have to hold non-financial instruments for a longer period of time to make money. Also, converting non-financial investments to cash quickly is not always possible.

Non-financial investments include things such as real estate, art, stamps, coins, cars, or just about anything else that people feel will rise in value. I normally place all of these investments in the moderate to high risk category because there is always a chance that you will lose money rather than make it. Even a real estate investment, while being relatively safe, doesn't guarantee untold wealth. Many people lose money on real estate deals because the property value doesn't rise as expected and may actually decline in value. This occurred in the early 2000's throughout the United States.

The major thing to keep in mind is that real estate, art, stamps, etc. are only worth what people are willing to pay. The price that a person is willing to pay for an item is normally based on the item's scarcity and its perceived value. The item's value is quite often determined by how many people want the same thing and how badly they want it.

The greater the number of people who want an item, the more it will tend to cost. I once attended a police auction and watched people bid on an old bicycle. If the same bicycle was new and sold in a store, it would have cost around $70, but this one sold for $90. I later asked a few of the bidders why they were willing to pay so much for an old bicycle when they could have gotten a new one for less. Some  said that they just got caught up in the spirit of the bidding. However, most of the people I spoke to said that the bicycle was the only one at the auction and they wanted it. Scarcity is the reason why the price of many goods increases in value:

- During the 1980's, after Coca Cola announced that it was changing the formula of its popular soft drink (now called Coca Cola Classic), the price of a case of the soda sold for up to $50 in some places. The reason that people were paying so much for the drink was not because the taste was so great, it was because people knew that there would be no more, and therefore felt that it would be a collector's item. Obviously, when Coke put the old formula back on the market, all of the people who speculated in the Coke market lost.

- When a lot of people want to borrow money from banks, but only a small amount of money is available to lend, the cost to borrow (the interest rate) goes up. In contrast, when money is more readily available, interest rates go down.

- Companies that produce items such as handcrafted plates or cars often make "limited edition" series that are numbered and come with a certificate showing that the item is one of a limited series. By doing so, the producers charge a higher price for the items and consumers are usually willing to pay the higher amount if they feel the piece will rise in price as a collector's Item. (Of course, the producers never guarantee that it will rise.)

- There are only a few companies in the world that produce diamonds. To make sure that the value of diamonds remain high, the companies greatly limit the amount that are distributed on the world market. Also, they spend a lot of money telling consumers that diamonds are valuable.

The secret to making money in any non-financial investment, just like with the financial ones, is to read and ask questions. Pick a category of investment in which you're interested and become an "expert". You should learn the subject inside and outside. If you don't have the time or desire to do this, then you should hire someone who knows the area of investment well. Once you've done either one of these two things, and with some luck, you just might make money.

Investments Illustrated

The following table shows the investments that are discussed in this book. It has been provided to give you an overall comparison of the different investments that will be covered. Since most readers are familiar with savings accounts offered by banks, each investment is compared to a savings account, which means that the return on investment, risk, and liquidity for a savings account is considered average, and the other investments are rated either above or below that type of investment account.

Investment Table

Investment Vehicle	Risk	Potential ROI	Liquidity	Initial Capital Outlay
Savings Accounts	2	1	5	~ $10
Certificates of Deposit	2	1 to 2	3	$1000 or more
Treasury Bills	1	2	4	variable
Treasury Notes	1	2	3	$1000 or more
Treasury Bonds	1	2	3	$1000 or more
Money Market Funds	2	2	5	$100 to $5000*
Municipal Bonds	2	2	3	$1000 or more
Brokerage Instruments	3	2	4	variable
Credit Union Accts	2	1	5	~ $5
Common Stock	3 to 4	3 to 5	4	$100 or more
Corporate Bonds	3	2	3	$100 or more
Preferred Stock	3	3	4	$1000 or more
Commercial Paper	3	2	4	$250 or more
Mutual Funds	3 to 4	3 to 4	4	$100 to $5000*
Unit Investment Trusts	3 to 4	3 to 4	4	$100 or more
Limited Partnerships	4 to 5	3 to 4	1	$500 or more
Commodities	5	4 to 5	4	$500 or more*
Options	5	3 to 5	4	$500 or more**
Foreign Currency	5	3 to 5	4	$500 or more

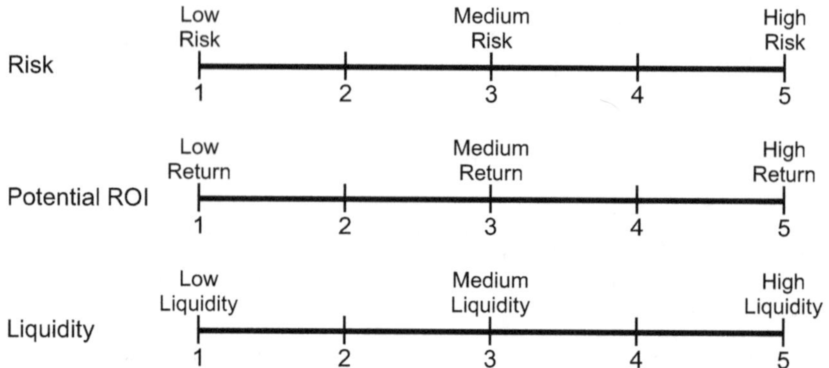

The following are definitions of the terms and symbols used on the chart:

TERMS

Investment Vehicle - An investment vehicle, unlike a motor vehicle, will not take you from place to place. However, it is the type of investment that you decide to use when attempting to make money. Of course, if you choose a good investment vehicle, you can buy a motor vehicle to go from place to place.

Risk -This is what you take whenever you make an investment *(some people also take Valium)*. The risk is the amount of chance you take of losing some or all of your investment.

Return on Investment (ROI) - This represents how much money you make from deciding which path represents truth, justice and the American way. Some instruments have more than one number because the ROI depends on the particular investment.

Liquidity - This indicates how quickly and easily you can turn the money you've invested back into cash. If you can get cash from an investment within a twenty-four hour period, it is considered very liquid. If you must wait years to get your money - your investment may be solid, but you are not liquid. As with the ROI, liquidity can vary depending on the investment.

Initial Capital Outlay - This is the money that you must put out in order to invest.

SYMBOLS

~ This symbol means "approximately".

* Although this varies from $100 to $5,000, the normal range is between $1,000 and $5,000.

** The investment requirements depend on the type of transaction, of which there are many.

! The risk depends on the kind of stock.

An Amazing Girl Named Grace

This begins the continuing adventures of Grace Vest. Grace is a very enterprising young lady. At the age of six she earned her first 25¢ when she was paid to leave the room by her older sister's boyfriend. After experiencing the initial excitement from earning that first quarter, Grace knew that making money was in her blood. She began spending as much time around her sister as possible so she could be paid to leave the area. Also, whenever her sister got a new boyfriend, Grace made an effort to check his financial statement and credit history.

Grace knew that the opportunity to collect from her sister's boyfriends would not last forever. She also knew that earning money 25¢ at a time would take a lot of patience. She had no patience because she wasn't a doctor. Since her first encounter with the wonders of making money, Grace has held many jobs, which included baby sitter; lemonade seller; grass cutter; newspaper carrier and delivery person. She has also tried her hand at being an artist, which had its drawbacks; an elevator operator, which had its ups and downs; and a locksmith, which she really couldn't get into.

Until now she has put all of her money into her socks. When a sock was full, Grace stuffed it in her mattress. Because of her desire to see her money grow faster and because she was running out of socks to wear, Grace decided that her mattress was not the answer. Grace then began thinking about the different types of financial instruments in which she can invest.

Come journey with Grace into the land of financial investments, where millions *(or at least hundreds)* can be made or lost just because it began raining in some part of the world or because a certain individual was hired or fired.

Chapter 2
-- Low Risk Investments

This chapter describes some of the low risk investments in which you can place your money. The term "low risk" simply means that you can invest in these instruments and go to bed secure with the feeling that, as long as Congress does not decide to change the currency from dollars to rutabagas; the Federal Reserve Bank doesn't recall all of the money because of defective ink; or Kim Jong-un isn't elected President of the United States, you will not lose the total amount that you invest. Not worrying about your money allows you to worry about other important things such as why isn't a banana called a "yellow" since an orange is called an "orange."

Although this thought of safety can give you a warm feeling inside, as with all things in life, except possibly a lifetime supply of confortable shoes, low risk investments do have certain disadvantages. With this in mind, we will now venture forth with Grace and look at some of the safest areas of investment available.

Bank Instruments

Unlike pianos, flutes and other musical instruments, most bank instruments do not make a sound. However, both bank and musical instruments do have a few things in common:

- With both you can make money, which can be music to your ears.

- You don't have to have a great deal of training to begin using either of them.

- The more you learn about how they both function, the more proficient you become at using them.

- The more experienced a player becomes, the greater the amount of money the person can usually make.

Grace is considering putting her money into a savings account and a certificate of deposit.

Savings Accounts

Savings accounts are probably one of the oldest and most well known methods of making money. From the time we start earning money from paper routes and baby-sitting, our parents suggest, if not demand, that we open a savings account. Although at that age we are usually more concerned about all of the things that we absolutely need, like a new video game, or the rest of the Power Ranger or Barbie collection, having money in your own bank account can give a child the feeling of becoming an adult. Since this form of saving is normally the first one brought to our attention, it is, perhaps, the one that comes to mind first whenever we think about saving. When you add to this the constant advertisements by banks, there is no wonder that when a person has a bit of extra money, he immediately runs to the nearest bank.

The amount of interest paid by banks is not a fixed rate -- it can change at any time. In recent years, banks have been paying approximately 3% interest, which is compounded quarterly. The term "compounded quarterly" means that every three months, interest is added to the money that you originally put into the account (the principle), and interest is then paid on the new amount. One misconception some people have is that the full 3% is added to their account every three months. That is not true. The 3% rate is the annual rate - the total percentage paid over a one year period. If the annual rate is three percent, the actual rate paid each quarter is about 0.75%, which is 3% divided by four.

If, on January 1, Grace deposits $1,000 into a savings account that pays 3% interest, on April 1 she will receive $7.50 interest. The $7.50 interest is calculated by multiplying Grace's $1,000 by

0.75% (.0075), which is the interest rate, paid in the first three months. She then has $1007.50 in her savings account.

By letting her money stay in the account for a year, she will receive the following:

Date	Interest
April 1	$7.50
July 1	$7.56
October 1	$7.61
January 1	$7.67
Total Interest	**$30.34**

This means that Grace will have a total of $1,030.34 in her savings account at the end of the year.

If Grace lets her money stay in her savings account for four additional years and doesn't make any deposits or withdrawals, on January 1 of the sixth year, she will have $1,161.18.

It is very important to take note that in the previous example I did not simply multiply $1,000 by 3%. If I had done that, at the end of the first year Grace would have received $30 in interest, instead of $30.34. At the end of the fifth year, rather that receiving $161.18, she would have only gotten $159.27. The reason for the big difference in the amounts is because in each case the smaller amounts represent **simple interest.** Simple interest means that you are paid interest only on the money that you deposit:

*Scarlet O'Hara deposits $1,000 into an account paying 3% **compounded** interest. At the end of the first three months she receives $7.50 interest. Her account now has $1,007.50. In the second three months she will receive $7.56 in interest. This amount is interest being paid on the total amount in the account, not just the amount that Scarlet originally deposited. During the six month period, Miss Scarlet earned a total of $15.06.*

> *Rhett Butler deposits $1,000 into an account paying 3% simple interest. At the end of the first three months he receives $7.50 interest. His account now has $1,007.50. In the second three months he will again receive $7.50 interest. This amount is interest being paid only on the amount that he deposited in the account, not on the total amount in the account. During the same six month period, Rhett only received $15.00.*

A few dollars of interest may not seem like a lot when investing a small amount of money. However, whether you receive simple or compound interest can have a much greater impact as you invest more money. Had Scarlet and Rhett deposited $1,000,000 rather than $1,000, in the second three months they would have earned $7,560 and $7,500, respectively. Besides, if you can earn an extra penny or two, why not do it?

Although saving accounts may not be the best place for Grace to put her money, there are some instances when an account of this type is practical. One such case is when she needs quick access to cash during those times when banks are closed. In a situation such as this, a savings account and an automatic teller card can be as popular as an umbrella in a rain storm. Also, if Grace wants to invest in another type of instrument, but does not have enough money at the time, a savings account is a way of saving until she has the needed funds, Even though the interest she receives is not as high as other investments, she will earn more interest in the bank than in her mattress *(unless her mattress is also in the bank).*

SAVINGS ACCOUNTS

ADVANTAGES	
Extremely Safe	The Federal Depository Insurance Corporation (F.D.I.C.) insures accounts up to a set limit. This guarantees that you will get at least the insured portion of your money even if the bank goes out of business.
No Minimum Deposit	In most cases, you can open an account with as little as $10.00.
Quick Access to Money	In addition to having longer hours during the week, some banks also have Saturday hours. Additionally, the ATM and debit card system makes it possible to shop, deposit or withdraw money 24 hours a day.
DISADVANTAGES	
Low Rate of Return	There are many other Investments with higher rates of return and that provide many of the same services as banks.
Service Charge	If an account does not have a minimum balance set by the institution, some banks will impose a service charge.

Certificates of Deposit

Certificates of Deposit (CD's) are fixed income instruments issued by state banks, national banks, and state or federal savings and loan associations. "Fixed income" means that, as long as you keep a CD, you will receive the specified interest. Interest paid by CDs varies depending on the financial institution and the prevailing interest rate. While most institutions make interest payments semiannually (twice a year), some pay monthly, quarterly, annually, or when the certificate matures. One primary difference between a Certificate of Deposit and a savings account is that a higher rate of interest is paid on the certificates. The reason for the higher interest is because they are "time deposits". That means that Grace must keep her money in the account for a specified amount of time. If she wants the get her money back from the bank early, she will be penalized.

Since banks aren't allowed to send Grace to bed without her supper, nor can they break her knee caps (legally), they will penalize her by paying her less if she removes the money early. Moreover, if Grace needs her money in a hurry, there is still no guarantee that she could get it as quickly as she wishes.

Another major difference is that you must invest the total amount at one time. In contrast, with a savings account you can normally deposit any amount you wish at any time. Certificates of Deposit can be purchased in various amounts, and have different maturity dates. The dates indicate the length of time you must wait before you can get your money and interest without being penalized. The period is based on your specific desires. It can be seven days, thirty days, ninety days, six months, or a number of other periods.

Usually, the longer it takes for the certificate to mature, which means that your money is tied up for a greater period of time, the higher the interest rate you will be paid. Although the interest rate is fixed on certificates of deposit with a given maturity date, the same type of CD with a different maturity date will not necessarily pay the same rate.

Grace has $2,000 to invest, but she doesn't want all of her money tied up for a long time. Therefore, with $1,000 she decides to buy a certificate of deposit that matures in thirty days. Since it has a short maturity period, the CD only pays 5% interest. With the other$1,000, Grace buys another CD that matures in ninety days. The second certificate will pay 5.5% interest.

At the end of thirty days the first certificate will mature, and Grace will receive $1,004.16, which represents the original amount of her investment, plus the 5% interest paid for the thirty day period. (Remember, the 5% interest rate is the rate paid for a full year. By letting her money sit for only thirty days she received one-twelfth of that, or .416%.)

At the end of ninety days the second certificate of deposit will mature, and Grace will receive $1,013.75. This amount represents the original amount of her second investment, plus the 5.5% interest paid for the ninety day period.

Since there is a difference between the interest rate of a thirty-day and a ninety-day certificate of deposit, if she does not need *her money extremely fast, Grace is better off buying one ninety-day certificate rather than buying three thirty-day certificates. The ninety-day CD made $13.75, while the three thirty-day ones would only earn $12.48.*

Certificates of Deposit are a place for Grace to put her money if she doesn't feel that she will need it very quickly. However, if she wants to get a higher interest rate while still having relatively quick access to her money, Grace should consider buying CDs with short maturity periods. Then, when the certificates mature, she can buy more certificates with short maturity periods. Although Grace will not receive an interest rate as high as if she bought CDs with longer maturity periods, she will be getting a rate higher that a regular savings account, plus she will have some flexibility.

The Certificate of Deposit Secondary Market

Unknown to most people, a secondary market exists in the wonderful world of CDs. When a person buys a Certificate of Deposit from a bank, that person is buying it in the **primary market.** In other words, it is a newly issued certificate -- no one has owned it previously. As I previously stated, if Grace wanted to get her money before her CD matures, there would be a penalty. However, rather than returning it back to the bank, it may be possible for her to sell it m the secondary market.

The secondary market is a place where people who want to sell their certificates can sell them to people who want to buy CDs, which is similar to trading stock in the stock market. The price of a Certificate of Deposit traded in the secondary market will depend on the prevailing market conditions and interest rates. Therefore, they might sell for a price equal to, greater than or less than the original price. CDs in the secondary market are normally purchased through full-service stock brokerage firms. This gives buyers and sellers throughout the country the ability to reach people that they could not ordinarily reach. CDs in the secondary market come in a wide variety of maturities and coupon payments, which means the buyers often have a much larger selection of products than if they buy directly from banks.

Bud Lyte buys a five-year $1,000 Certificate of Deposit paying 7% interest from his local bank in St. Louis. Since the certificate

*pays semiannually, every six months Bud will receive $35.
Eighteen months before the CD matures. Bud decides that he no
longer wants it. However, because he bought it directly from the
bank, it must be cashed in at the bank. Therefore, a penalty will
be assessed by the bank.*

*At the same time that Bud buys his CD, his brother Miller Lyte
buys a five-year $1,000 CD paying 7% interest issued by the
same bank in St Louis. However, he purchases it through a
brokerage house. Like his brother, Miller also decides that he
wants his money eighteen months before the CD matures. Since
it was purchased through a brokerage house, Miller contacts the
firm and has the representative offer the CD in the secondary
CD market.*

*Joe Camel, who is living in Fort Worth, Texas, decides that he
wants to buy a CD that matures in eighteen months. Since
Miller's CD is available, Joe has the ability to buy it through his
brokerage firm. However, current CD rates for an 18 month
period are 5% instead of 7%. As a result, rather than paying
$1,000 for the certificate, Joe will have to pay more. The reason
for this is because he will be receiving payments of $35 per
month when he should only be receiving $25 per month. To make
up for the extra $30 that he will be receiving ($10 times 3
payments), Joe will have to pay approximately $1,030 for the
CD. When it matures, Joe will receive $1,000.*

It is important to point out that, although you can buy CDs from
brokerage firms, brokerage houses do not actually issue them. CDs are
issued by banks and savings and loans.

CERTIFICATES OF DEPOSIT

ADVANTAGES	
Extremely Safe	As with savings accounts, the Federal Depository Insurance Corporation (F.D.I.C.) insures the certificates.
Interest Rate	Certificates of Deposits pay a reasonably good interest rate in comparison to some other investments.
DISADVANTAGES	
Slow Access to Money	In order to receive the interest guaranteed to you by the financial institution, your money must be left in the account until the maturity date.
Deposit Required to Invest	The minimum deposit required to invest in a Certificate of Deposit is usually no less than $1,000.
Penalty for Early Withdrawal	The federal government requires banks to assess depositors a penalty for withdrawing their money from a Certificate of Deposit before the maturity date.

U.S. Government Instruments

U.S. Government instruments are not musical instruments played by  members of congress, nor are they surgical instruments used by the president to dissect the federal budget. They are financial instruments offered by the federal government in which you can invest. Many foreign governments, large banks and other institutional investors have at least a portion of their investment in some type of government instrument. One of the major reasons they do so is because the instruments are considered very safe.

The three major investment opportunities offered, which are also the ones Grace will consider, are Treasury Bills, Treasury Notes and Treasury Bonds.

Treasury Bills

Treasury Bills (T-Bills) are a form of promissory note (I.O.U.) issued by the United States federal government through the Federal Reserve Bank. They are short-term loans to the government that usually mature in thirteen weeks, twenty-six weeks or fifty-two weeks. The T-Bill's maturity depends on what is requested by the buyer from the Federal Reserve Bank. Normally, the longer the maturity date, the more interest you will receive.
Treasury Bills are normally sold in minimum amounts of $10,000, and in multiples of $5,000 above that. If you don't happen to have an extra $10,000 lying around, don't despair, you can buy them in smaller amounts from banks or brokers. Of course, since banks and brokers never do things out of the goodness of their hearts, you must pay a fee to buy the bills using that method. Doing so reduces the amount you actually make, but it can still be a worth while investment.

The $10,000 and $5,000 values of Treasury Bills are called the "face value". That is, if you actually held one in your hand, or if someone else held one in their hand, like regular currency, the bill would have their full value printed on its face. If you buy Treasury Bills, you will pay an amount lower than the face value. The price you actually pay is called the **discount rate.**

From the time that a Treasury Bill is first issued by the government, until the time it matures, no interest payments are made. The way that the federal government pays interest on the bills is by selling them at a discount rate, and then paying the face amount at maturity.

> *Grace decides to buy a Treasury Bill that will pay her 5% interest and matures in fifty-two weeks. Rather than paying $10,000 for the bill and receiving $500 in interest payments, she will pay $9,493 for the bill. At maturity she will receive $10,000. The difference between what she paid for the bill and what she will receive when the bill matures, which is $507, represents the interest.*

Treasury Bills are auctioned by the Federal Reserve Bank on a regular schedule. The thirteen and twenty-six week bills are auctioned each week, the fifty-two week bills are offered every four weeks. If Grace wishes to purchase Treasury bills, she can do so as either a competitive or a non-competitive bidder. Whether she is a competitive bidder or a non-competitive bidder depends on the amount of Treasury Bills she wants to buy. All competitive bidders must buy more than $500,000 worth of bills. Although the competitive bidders are normally banks, money market funds and other large institutions, Grace can place a competitive bid if she wishes. However, since her socks don't currently hold $500,000, let's assume that she will be investing less than that amount, which means she will be a non-competitive bidder.

By submitting a non-competitive bid, Grace is assured of receiving the amount of bills she wants to buy. After all of the non-competitive bidders get what they want, the remainder of the bills is sold to the competitive bidders starting with the bidders that were willing to accept the lowest amount of interest.

To purchase a Treasury Bill, Grace must submit both a bid form, called a "tender" and a check for $10,000 to the Federal Reserve Bank. All of this must be sent in before the government begins auctioning the bills. Once the auction is complete, the discount rate that Grace will pay as a non-competitive bidder is calculated. The rate is the average price of all of the competitive bids that were accepted.

If the discounted price is $9,600, once the auction is over, the bank will send her a check for $400 and a receipt. The $400 represents the difference between the $10,000 she sent and the discount price. When the bill matures, she will be sent a check for $10,000. However, if she fills out a form to have the money "rolled over" (reinvested), she will receive a check for the difference between $10,000 and the new Treasury Bill rate.

Once she becomes the proud owner of a Treasury Bill, the United States Treasury Department will open an account in her name, and they will make a **book entry.** The book entry means that, rather than actually receiving an engraved certificate, Grace will receive a receipt to prove that she bought a Treasury Bill. By handling the transaction that way, the government keeps the purchaser from having to worry about the certificate being lost or stolen. Also, by using book entries to record the selling of Treasury Bills the government has put a lot of counterfeiters out of work, as well as eliminating the expense involved in printing and engraving the certificates.

TREASURY BILLS

ADVANTAGES	
Extremely Safe	As long as the federal government stays in business, you can feel confident that you will receive both your money and interest.
No State or Local Taxes	While federal taxes must be paid on interest received, you are exempt from paying state and local taxes.
Reasonably Good Interest Rate	Although the interest rate varies with each issuance of bills, the rate you receive is normally good when considering the fact that Treasury Bills are short-term obligations, very safe and no state or local taxes are paid.
DISADVANTAGES	
Large Investment Required	The minimum amount needed to invest in Treasury Bills is $10,000, which is higher than many other investments. You can, however, invest in bills through banks or brokers for less money, but a fee will be charged.
Cannot Get Money Quickly	While you can get your money out in a reasonably fast time, you may have to wait until the maturity date unless they are bought and sold through a brokerage firm.

Treasury Notes

Treasury Notes are another form of I.O.U. issued by the United States federal government through the Federal Reserve Bank. Unlike Treasury Bills, they take much longer to mature. Treasury Notes have maturity periods that range from one to ten years. The maturity of the notes depends on what the government wishes to issue at a given time. Grace can buy them in denominations of $1,000 or $5,000.

Treasury Notes are auctioned by the Federal Reserve Bank on a irregular schedule throughout the year. If Grace wants to buy the notes, just like Treasury Bills, she can buy them either as a competitive bidder or as a non-competitive bidder. As in the case of Treasury Bills, the competitive bidders are normally banks, money market funds and other large institutions.

Grace has the right to place a competitive bid for notes if she has the desire and at least $1,000,000. There is no maximum amount that she can buy. Of course, there is also no guarantee that she will be able to get all of the Treasury Notes that she wants if she tries to buy them as a competitive bidder. Like Treasury Bills, all competitive bidders are competing against each other for the notes. *(That's probably why it's called a competitive bid.)* If she wants to be a non-competitive bidder, she cannot buy any more than $1,000,000 worth of the notes. By buying the lesser amount, Grace is assured of receiving the amount of notes she wants.

Depending on the bid, the price of Treasury Notes can be less than, equal to or greater than the face value of the certificate. Unlike Treasury Bills, from the time that a Treasury Note is first issued by the government, until the time that it matures, interest payments are made every six months. When the Treasury Notes mature, purchasers will also receive the face value of the notes.

To buy Treasury Notes as a non-competitive bidder, Grace must submit both a bid form and a check equal to the face amount of the notes to the Federal Reserve Bank. If the bid price is greater than the face value of the note, she must send the bank the extra money. *(For example, If the bid price is $11,000, the Grace must send in the extra $1,000.)* If the price of the note is less than the amount she originally sent in, the bank will send her a check for the difference between the actual cost of the note and the amount she sent.

Whether Grace purchases the notes at a higher price, a lower price or the same price as the face value, she will receive interest payments every six months until the notes mature. At maturity, she will receive the face value of the notes.

TREASURY NOTES

ADVANTAGES	
Extremely Safe	Since Treasury Notes are sold by the U.S. Government, they are one of the safest investments available.
No State or Local Taxes	You only pay federal tax on the interest you receive -- no state or local taxes are assessed.
Good Rate of Return	The interest rate, while being different from issue to issue, is normally good and sometimes better than other non tax-exempt long term notes.
Semi-annual Interest Payments	You receive a steady stream of interest payments every six months for the duration of the bond.
DISADVANTAGES	
Slow Access to Your Money	Depending on the maturity date, you may have to wait from one to ten years before getting the initial amount of your investment back unless the notes are bought and sold through a brokerage firm.
Sold at Irregular Intervals	You cannot use Treasury Notes as part of a regular investment strategy because they are issued at irregular intervals.

Treasury Bonds

Treasury Bonds are a third form of I.O.U. issued by the federal government through the Federal Reserve Bank. Just like Treasury Notes, bonds take a long time to mature. Maturity normally takes ten years or more depending on what the government decides to issue. They are auctioned by the Federal Reserve Bank on an irregular schedule throughout the year and can be bought in denominations of $1,000 and $5,000.

If Grace wants to be bonded she can do so as either a competitive or a non-competitive bidder. Being a competitive bidder means that she will be bidding against the big institutions and banks, she must have at least $1,000,000 to compete and she may not be able to purchase the amount of bonds she wants. If Grace is a little low on cash when the government offers the bonds or she wants to be assured of getting the amount of bonds she wants, she can buy them as a non-competitive bidder. As a non-competitive bidder, she can't buy more than $1,000,000 worth. All she has to do is submit a bid form and a check.

Like Treasury Notes, the price she must pay for Treasury Bonds can be less than, equal to or greater than the face value of the certificate. If the price is greater than the face value, she must send in the extra money. If it is less, the Federal Reserve Bank will send her a check for the difference between the discounted bond rate and the amount she sent. Whether she purchases the bonds at a higher price, a lower price or the same price as the face value, Grace will receive interest every six months until the bond matures. At maturity, she will receive the face value of the bond.

TREASURY BONDS

ADVANTAGES	
Extremely Safe	Treasury Bonds, being financial an instrument sold by the U.S. Government, are a very safe form of investment.
No State or Local Taxes	You only pay federal tax on the interest you receive -- no state or local taxes are assessed.
Good Rate of Return	The interest rate, while being different from issue to issue, is normally good, and sometimes better than other non tax-exempt long term notes.
Semi-annual Interest Payments	You receive a steady stream of interest payments every six months for the duration of the bond.
DISADVANTAGES	
Slow Access to Your Money	Depending on the maturity date, you may have to wait for ten years or more before getting the initial amount of your investment back unless the notes are bought and sold through a brokerage firm.
Sold at Irregular Intervals	You cannot use Treasury Bonds as part of a regular investment strategy because they are issued at irregular intervals.

The Government Bond Secondary Market

I have found that many people choose to not buy government notes and bonds because they believe that the instruments must be held until they mature. However, as with CDs, there exists a secondary market for U.S. government bills, notes and bonds. This means that, although a person who buys a government instrument cannot receive their money back from the federal government before it matures, they can possibly sell it to someone else in the secondary market. Also, if a person wants to buy a bond, but not hold it for ten years or more, they have that opportunity by using secondary market. In fact, the secondary market is a very good way to develop an investment strategy using bonds.

Money Market Funds

Money Market Funds are similar to savings accounts because you normally have quick access to your money. However, they are different because of the types of instruments in which they invest and the type of companies that offer them. Money market funds invest in short-term instruments such as Commercial Paper, Certificates of Deposit, Eurodollar Certificates of Deposit, Banker's Acceptances, Taxable Floaters and short-term U.S. government securities. This means that the assets held by the funds are very liquid. Depending on her investment strategy Grace must decide which is right for her. The investments of money market funds normally fall into one of three categories:

- Funds that invest only in short-term municipal bonds, which might be tax free.
- Funds that invest only in short-term U.S. Government securities, which might be free of state and local taxes.
- Funds that invest in other short-term instruments such as commercial paper and certificates of deposit, which are fully taxable.

The funds are offered by banks and investment companies. Each fund has its own requirements for investing in them, which include the following:

- **Minimum amount required to invest** -- There is no set amount that you must invest in money market funds. Each fund sets its own requirements. Some let you start out with as little as $100, while other might require as much as $500,000, or more.

- **Interest earned** -- Although most money market funds invest in the same types of short-term instruments, the interest that is paid out to investors can be quite different. You should check on the interest being paid by a fund prior to selecting it.

- **Check writing privileges** -- While most funds offer you the ability to write checks, they do not have the same privileges. Some funds allow you to write as many checks as you want for any amount. With other funds, checks cannot be written for less than a set amount - for example $500. Additionally, some funds limit the number of checks that can be written within a certain period of time. The fact that the number of checks you can write might be limited, you will still be able to get your money by contacting the fund and having them send you a check.

Money market funds are a good place for Grace to keep the portion of her money that she wants to remain liquid. However, I do not recommend keeping everything in this type of fund because it will not grow very quickly.

MONEY MARKET FUNDS

ADVANTAGES	
Extremely Safe	Since money market funds invest In a variety of short-term instruments, you can feel confident that your money will be there when you need it.
Small Investment	In some cases, you can open an account with as little as $100, or less.
Quick Access to Money	You can get your money quickly by simply writing a check, or calling the fund and requesting that a check be sent or wired into your bank account.
DISADVANTAGES	
Low Rate of Return	While many money market accounts normally pay a higher rate than savings accounts, the return is not as good as other investments.
Access to Your Money	If the fund that you use limits the check amount or number of checks you can write during a certain period, you may not be able to get your money as quickly as you need it.

Municipal Bonds

Municipal Bonds, like U.S. government bonds, are debt obligations (I.O.U.s). However, instead of being issued by the federal government, they are offered by states or any legally recognized political subdivision of a state. Examples of political subdivisions include cities, counties, school districts, public hospitals, and bridge and tunnel authorities. Municipal bonds are also issued by the territories of Guam, the U.S. Virgin Islands, the commonwealth of Puerto Rico and the District of Columbia. Bonds are usually issued by municipalities when they need money for a project. By issuing bonds, rather than increasing taxes of the people who live in the area, a municipality is borrowing money from people throughout the country. However, in some cases the citizens in the area where the bonds are issued are paying back the interest in the form of taxes.

Interest received from most municipal bonds is exempt from federal income tax as long as the bonds are issued for traditional governmental purposes such as roads, municipal buildings and other capital projects. Moreover, if Grace buys a bond from a municipality in her own state, she may not have to pay state income tax either. The interest that is earned from bonds issued by U.S. territories such as Guam, U.S. Virgin Islands, Puerto Rico and American Samoa is exempt from all income tax.

Unlike U.S. government bonds that are guaranteed by the full faith and credit of the federal government, municipal bonds are rated by Moody's and Standard & Poor's. The ratings can be as high as Aaa from Moody's and AAA from Standard and Poor's, to as low as no rating (NR). The rating is based on the municipality's ability to repay the principal and make the interest payments. The rating that a bond receives is based on whether they are insured by one of the bond insurance companies and the type of bond being issued. When a bond is insured, the insurer agrees to pay all interest and principal if the issuer fails to pay the costs for any reason. Currently, the American Municipal Bond Assurance Corporation (AMBAC), the Municipal Bond Investors Assurance Corporation (MBIAC), the Financial Guarantee Insurance Company (FGIC) and the Bond Investors Guaranty Insurance Company (BIG) are the largest issuers of bonds insurance. Both Moody's and Standard and Poor's assign the highest rating to bonds that are insured.

The type of bond issued can affect both the bond's rating and whether it is totally exempt from federal income tax. The types of bonds issued by municipalities are described below:

>**General Obligation Bonds (GOs)** are secured by the full
>faith, credit and taxing power of the entity issuing it.
>Therefore, the only type of entity that can issue a GO bond is
>one with the ability to levy and collect taxes. State
>governments can issue GO bonds since they collect income,
>sales, gasoline excise and other taxes. Counties and cities can
>also issue general obligation bonds since they assess things
>such as property taxes.

>**Revenue Bonds** are issued to finance various types of projects.
>The revenue generated from the project is used to pay the
>bondholders the interest and principal. Just a few of the types
>of revenue bonds are described below:

- <u>Housing revenue bonds</u> are issued by state or local housing finance agencies to help finance single family or multi-family housing.

- <u>Utility revenue bonds</u> are used to finance gas, water and sewer, and electric power systems that are owned by the local government. The fees charged to customers and any excess power sold to large public utilities is used to pay principal and interest.

- <u>Health Care revenue bonds</u> are used for the construction of nonprofit hospitals and health care facilities. The gross revenue generated by the facility is normally used to pay principal and interest.

- <u>Transportation bonds</u> are used to finance projects such as tunnels, toll roads, bridges, airports and transit systems. The fees collected from users are used to pay the bondholders.

As I previously mentioned, the interest from many, but not all municipal bonds are free from federal income tax. However, any capital gains earned from the sale or redemption of municipal bonds is not free from federal tax. The following example will illustrate the difference between interest and capital gains.

In 1985, Kermit T. Frog, who lives in California, purchased a 15-year, $1,000 State of California general obligation bond that pays 8% interest. Every six months, Kermit receives a $40 interest payment, which is free from federal income tax. Also, since he is a resident of California, he will not have to pay California state income tax on the interest.

During 1995, Kermit decides to sell the bond. George O. T. Jungle, who also lives in California, decides to buy the bond. However, the interest rate for municipal bonds is only 5%. Since the coupon on the bond is 8%, and George is only supposed to receive 5% interest, he has to pay a premium for the bond. If he keeps the bond until it matures, he will receive $400 ($80 per year times 5 years). However, because of the current interest rate, George is only supposed to receive $250. Therefore, he must pay $1,150 to cover the additional money he will be receiving, but will only receive $1,000 when the bond matures.

As a result of these transactions, Kermit has received a $150 capital gain (profit), so he must pay federal and state taxes on the gain. However, although George must pay $1,150 for the bond, but will only receive $1,000 at maturity, he cannot claim a $150 loss because he has not actually loss any money. He will not have to pay federal or state tax on the interest payments that he receives.

Dudley D. Right, who lives in Montana, also decides to buy a California general obligation bond with a coupon that pays 4% interest. If he holds the bond until it matures, Dudley will receive $200 in interest payments. However, just like George, he should receive $250. In order to compensate for the interest that he will not be receiving, rather than paying $1,000 for the bond, Dudley will only have to pay $950. Dudley will not have to pay federal income tax on the $250 of interest payments, but he may have to pay Montana state tax because it is not a Montana bond. Additionally, since he only paid $950 for the bond, and will be receiving $1,000 when it matures, Dudley will have to pay federal and state tax on the $50 capital gain.

Municipal bonds, while being a relatively save investment, is not for everyone. They are usually more attractive to investors who are in a high tax bracket because the potential tax savings. In order to ascertain if tax free bonds are a good choice, Grace must determine whether she can make more money by investing in a taxable bond or a tax-free municipal bond.

John E. B. Good is a musician living in California who earns $30,000 per year. John's friend Karen, who also lives in California, earns $300,000 per year. They are both considering buying either a $5,000 municipal bond paying 5% interest, which means that they will both receive $250 tax free interest per year or a taxable bond paying 8% interest, which results in $400 of taxable income. Earning $30,000 per year places John in the 33.7% tax bracket (28% federal tax and 5.7% state tax). Karen's earnings of $300,000 place her in the 45.2% tax bracket (39.6% federal tax and 5.6% state tax). If John buys the taxable 8% bond, after taxes he will be able to keep $265.20. However, if Karen purchases the same bond, after taxes she will have only $219.20. Therefore, John will be better off if he buys the taxable *bond, but Karen will make more money if she purchases the tax-free municipal bond.*

The example illustrates that Grace should not buy municipal bonds just because they are tax free. If she can find a taxable investment that will yield a higher rate of return after taxes, it might be a better idea to buy the taxable one.

The Municipal Secondary Market

As with other fixed-income instruments (certificates of deposit and U.S. government bonds), there is a very active secondary market for municipal bonds. The secondary market makes it easy for individuals to locate tax-free bonds throughout the United States. A key point that should be remembered when buying bonds from other states is that while most bonds are free from federal tax, you may have to pay state or local tax.

A Word of Warning Regarding Municipal Bonds

Do not assume that all bonds issued by a municipality or that are issued for municipal projects are tax free and totally safe. Revenue bonds are issued to finance a specific project and pays interest from the money generated from that project. If the project does not make money, you might not receive the interest you expected to receive and there might be a problem getting you original investment back when the bonds mature. Also, make sure that the bonds are being issued by a government entity. Private companies can issue bonds for projects that will benefit the public, such as hospitals and parks. If a private company issues Revenue bonds, you might have to pay federal and state income tax on the interest that you receive.

Do not assume that a municipal bond is safe just because it issued by a government entity. The year 2013 marked a time when cities have begun filing for protection under the bankruptcy laws. Detroit, Michigan and San Bernardino, California have been two of the largest ones. If a city goes into bankruptcy, it is possible that you will lose all or a portion of your initial investment and/or the interest that you expected to receive.

MUNICIPAL BONDS

ADVANTAGES	
Safe	Depending on the rating of the bonds, you can feel confident that as long as you own the bonds, you will make money and not lose your principal investment.
Tax Free	You do not have to pay federal Income tax on many municipal bonds and may not pay state tax if they are issued by an entity within the state in which you live.
Small Investment	The amount required to invest in municipal bonds is relatively low.
Continuous Interest Payments	Many municipal bonds pay interest semiannually, which results in continuous payments for as long as you hold the bond.
DISADVANTAGES	
Lower Interest Rates	The interest rate on municipal bonds are normally lower than taxable bonds, which means that they might not be a good investment for people who are not in a high tax bracket.
Liquidity	If you need your money quickly and wish to sell the bond, you may not be able to sell it for the same price you paid.

Brokerage Instruments

Brokerage instruments are items such as TENTS; CATS and STRIPS, which have nothing to do with camping; felines or bacon. They are U.S. Government notes and bonds that have been modified by the stock brokerage or investment banking firm offering them. What the instruments are called depends solely on which firm offers them – JP Morgan calls them one thing, Merrill Lynch calls them another, and other companies call them something else.

As was mentioned in the section on government instruments, from the time treasury notes and bonds are first issued until the time they mature, interest payments are made every six months. At maturity, purchasers also receive the face value of the bond or note. Brokerage firms purchase the notes and bonds, modify them by "stripping" them of their coupons, and offer them to the public as "zero-coupon" instruments (zeros). This results in the buyer not getting any money until the instrument reaches maturity or until the buyer sells them to someone else.

The amount that the bonds are discounted depends on the interest rate being paid and the amount of time remaining before the bond matures. A bond paying five percent interest that matures in six months costs more than one paying the same rate, but having a maturity of ten years.

A key advantage with zero coupon instruments purchased through brokerage houses is that they are a lot more liquid than the original bond or note. That means you can buy them after the original date they were sold by the Federal Reserve Bank and can sell them before they mature, instead of having to wait until they mature. Also, because the brokerage firms continually buy the instruments, you can buy the "zeros" with a variety of maturity dates.

Grace is interested in buying a government bond because she feels that they are a safe investment. However, she does not want to send a check to the Treasury Department because she doesn't like not knowing how much interest she will receive until after the competitive bids are calculated, which is what happens by buying them through the Treasury Department as a non-competitive bidder. Also, she doesn't want to be forced to wait until they mature before she can realize a profit from the investment. Finally, Grace would rather pay a lower rate for the bond now, instead of receiving coupon payments every six months.

By electing to buy zero-coupon bonds from a brokerage house, all of her concerns are addressed. Rather than sending the full amount to the Treasury Department, she only pays the actual amount needed to make the purchase. Also, she knows exactly how much interest will be paid <u>before</u> the purchase is made, and can buy "zeros" that will mature when she needs them.

The preceding example illustrates that zero-coupon instruments can provide the safety of U.S. Government bonds and notes while giving you the flexibility of non-government instruments. Appendix E presents a method by which you can actually create your own bond by using "zeros".

BROKERAGE INSTRUMENTS

ADVANTAGES	
Safe	Since they are issued by the federal government, you can feel confident that you will receive your money at the end of the term.
Flexible	You can purchase the instruments with a wide variety of maturity dates. This means that you can determine when you will receive your money, and know exactly how much you will be receiving.
DISADVANTAGES	
Amount Required to Invest	Although the cost of investing in the instruments are lower than buying a coupon bond, brokerage firms normally set limits as to the minimum amount they will sell to an individual. This minimum may be more than you can afford.
Limited Access to Money	While you can determine when you will receive your money, if you need it sooner than originally planned, you may not be able to get it as quickly as you wish.

Credit Union Accounts

Credit unions are usually formed by people with something in common. This commonality can be anything from people who work at the same company or in the same kind of industry; to a group of left-handed people with acne. While there are many credit unions in existence, there is no guarantee that one has been formed by people in your profession or industry. After all, credit unions are only as strong its members. If there are not enough left-handed people with acne to create a base of members, the credit union will not have funds to lend, thereby not having adequate, funds with which to operate. The money that a credit union has to work with comes from deposits made by its members and from the interest it makes by investing or loaning that money out to its members.

> *Grace is a member of the Baby Sitters Credit Union (BSCU). Anyone who sits on babies can join. Each week she deposits $10.00 into her credit union account. Grace receives 4% interest, compounded quarterly, on her savings.*

> *Ana Thorne, another member of the Baby Sitters Credit Union, needs $800 so that she can buy living room furniture (she wanted something other than babies on which to sit). Although she could borrow the money from a bank or finance company, Ana decides to borrow it from the credit union because the interest rate is lower. Also, it is probably easier to borrow the money from the BSCU since she is a member.*

> *The credit union loans Ana the $800 at an interest rate of 12% and the circle is complete. That is, part of the money that Grace and other members have saved is being loaned to Ana. Ana pays 12% interest on her loan, Grace receives 4% interest on her savings and the credit union keeps the other 8% interest to cover its expenses.*

There are two primary ways that Grace can save with a credit union. One way is for her to deposit money in an account the same way she would in a bank account. The other, which is probably a lot more popular, is to have her employer automatically deduct the money from her paycheck and send it directly to the credit union. The second method, called **payroll deduction**, is more popular because she is able to save money without having to spend time and energy going to a bank. Also, having the money deducted automatically assures that it will get to the credit union, rather than the furniture or clothing stores that she might pass on the way.

More and more credit unions are setting themselves up like regular banks. They offer both checking and savings accounts, and provide Automatic Teller Machine (ATM) cards. Most credit unions also offer Visa and Master Cards to their members. As a result of these services, plus the fact that higher interest is paid on savings accounts and interest is also paid on checking accounts, many people are switching from banks to credit unions.

In the past, the biggest drawback with having a credit union account was their geographic inconvenience. That is, they were not as conveniently located as the major banks. Many credit unions still do not have a lot of locations in high rent areas, but they have begun linking up with other credit unions. As a result, members do not have to travel as far to conduct business. Also, credit union have teamed up with companies that place ATMs in convenience stores, which results in their members being able to withdraw their money without paying a fee to do so. The internet has also made credit unions more convenient. Now, a member can conduct transactions online and, in some instances, make deposits using their smart phones.

There is little risk involved in saving with a credit union. The only real risk is that it could become insolvent by making bad investments. The possibility is this occurring is smaller than banks since the loan committees are comprised of credit union members. These members are usually average working people who would not normally take extreme risks. After all, the reason for saving with a credit union in the first place is because it is a safe investment. Also, members of federally chartered credit unions are regulated by the National Credit Union Administration.

CREDIT UNION ACCOUNTS

ADVANTAGES	
Low Initial Investment	In most cases, a credit union account can be opened with a $5.00 deposit.
Quick Access to Money	They are normally open during regular business hours and some also have Saturday hours. Also, many credit unions have automatic teller machines, which make it possible to withdraw money 24 hours a day.
No Minimum Balance Required	Unlike banks, service charges are usually not imposed if there is a small amount in the account.
Direct Deposit Available	In many cases, your employer can send money directly to your account.
Wide Variety of Services	Some credit unions offer other services to its members such as free checking, loans with interest rates competitive to those of banks and credit cards with lower interest rates.
DISADVANTAGES	
Moderate Interest Paid	While they normally pay higher interest than regular savings accounts, the interest rate is still not great.
Not Federally Insured	Unlike banks, no organizations like the F.D.I.C. insure deposits. However, the National Credit Union Administration, a government agency, regulates all federally chartered credit unions.
Withdrawal Limitations	Some credit unions have a limitation on the number of times per month in which money can be withdrawn or transferred.

Chapter 3
-- Moderate Risk Investments

A "moderate risk" investment is one in which you can put your money and worry about losing your entire investment only during the times of a deep economic recession or depression. In other words, there is a risk of losing your money, but it is not extremely great. Moreover, the possibility of losing all of your investment overnight is even lower.

The primary difference between moderate and low risk investments are that, unlike many low risk investments, moderate risk investments are usually not insured by a federal agency. However, there are federal agencies that govern the operations of the firms involved with most of these investments.

Investment Stocks

I place stock into two main classifications - investment and speculative. This chapter will discuss investment stock and the next chapter will explain speculative stock.

Stock represents part ownership in a corporation. The amount of stock you own determines how much of the corporation you own. If there are a total of 100,000 shares of stock issued and Grace buys one share, then she owns 1/100,000th of the company - the more stock she owns, the more of the company she owns. All of the buildings, land, cash, equipment, etc. that a corporation possesses are owned by the stockholders. That does not mean that the stockholders have free use of them as they would their personal possessions. If the corporation goes out of business then all of the non-cash possessions of the corporation will be sold. Once all bills are paid, the stockholders will receive the remainder of the cash in proportion to the amount of stock owned.

A corporation's day-to-day operations are carried out by the firm's President and/or Chief Executive Officer (CEO). This person is an employee of the company and is hired indirectly by the stockholders. While it is the CEO who runs the corporation, the stockholders determine the firm's overall direction and major policies. This is accomplished by the stockholders voting on major issues. Each share of stock usually represents one vote. The more stock an individual owns, the more votes he has in determining policy.

Many very small corporations have only one stockholder who usually serves as the Chairman of the Board of Directors, President, Chief Executive Officer, Secretary, Treasurer and any other officer that is required. In cases like this, whenever a Board of Directors' or stockholder's meeting is held, either everyone is present or no one is there. Large corporations have thousands of stockholders. For all of these people to get together to decide the activities of the organization would be about as easy as getting a blue bonnet and a purple dress on an ostrich in a snow storm. Moreover, getting that many people to agree on any decision would be as difficult as getting Bill Clinton to admit he was just kidding when he said "... I never had intimate relations with that woman." To eliminate this problem, stockholders elect people to serve as members of the corporation's Board of Directors. The board is responsible for making the overall policies of the corporation. The President is normally hired by the Board and his activities are monitored by them. All people connected with the corporation are supposed to function in the best interest of the stockholders. Unfortunately, employees are sometimes more concerned about their own interests.

Unlike a magician's rabbit, stock does not appear out of thin air. If Grace wants to form a corporation and issue stock to the general public, she must do so in the following manner:

- **An individual, a group, or another corporation decides to form a corporation.** Grace must first decide in which state she wants to incorporate. Many small corporations are formed in the state where the incorporator lives; others are formed in a state different from the incorporator. The reason that some people incorporate in a state different from where they live is because some states, like Delaware and Nevada, have laws that are more advantageous to corporations - such as the corporations having to pay state tax only on money that is actually made in that state. *(Corporations in some states must pay state tax on money made anywhere in the world.)* Another reason could be that the principle business of the corporation will be in a different state.

Once she has decided on the state in which to incorporate, Grace must file documents with the government of that state. The document states the business the firm will be conducting, which in many cases is so general that the corporation is able to do anything legal. Also contained in the document is the number of shares of stock the company is issuing. After this is complete, the corporation can function as a legal entity, but cannot issue stock to the general public.

- **Forms are filed with the Securities and Exchange Commission (SEC) and other organizations.** Once she has officially formed the corporation, Grace must then file papers and submit documents to the Securities and Exchange Commission and other organizations such as Financial Industry Regulatory Authority (FINRA). These documents include requesting permission to sell stock to the general public and getting a trading symbol for the company. If permission is granted, the corporation can then start selling its stock on the open market.

Forming a corporation is very easy. Obtaining permission from the Securities and Exchange Commission to sell stock publicly is not easy. It takes a lot of time and money to do so. Moreover, if you are successful in getting permission to sell stock, there is absolutely no guarantee that someone will buy it. I have seen many companies offer stock to the public unsuccessfully. Many companies hire investment banking firms to help sell the new stock, but this still does not mean guaranteed success.

A corporation is viewed by the government as a legal entity. That means that it has its own tax identification (social security) number, must file income tax forms and must pay taxes based on its income. When a corporation is created, it begins with a certain amount of stock. Even though the person who formed the company might believe that she is the owner of all of the stock, until she actually purchases it from the corporation, she is not the owner.

Companies do not issue stock because the original stockholders have good hearts and want everyone to share in their good fortune. Stock is offered because money is needed for financing various projects or for general operating expenses. Stock can be issued directly by the company or sold by people who purchased it either from the firm or other individuals. When a company offers stock to the public for the first time it is called an **initial offering.**

Selling shares in this way increases the amount of cash with which the company has to work, but decreases the percentage of ownership held by the original stockholders. When stockholders resale their stock to other investors, the company doesn't receive any more money, nor is the percentage of ownership decreased. The sale of stock between investors, which is where most of the activity occurs, is called the "secondary market."

> *Grace forms a corporation that has 1,000 shares of stock and each share is worth $1.00. Grace buys 300 shares of stock from the corporation. The corporation now has 700 shares of stock and $300 of operating capital. Grace now owns 100% of the outstanding stock, which means she owns 100% of the company.*
>
> *The corporation needs more money to operate. The stockholders (Grace) decide that the corporation should sell 200 shares of stock to raise more money. The stockholders (Grace) have the first right to buy the 200 shares. However, she elects not to do so. Her second cousin Bill Board buys 100 shares and Bill's brother Chalk buys 100 shares. (Although Bill and Chalk bought stock for the same price as Grace, the price could have been higher or lower.)*
>
> *Now, the corporation has $500 in cash and 500 hundred shares of stock. Since 200 more shares were sold, Grace no longer owns 100% of the company - her stock has been diluted (even though she didn't add water). She now owns 60% of the company, Bill owns 20% of the company and Chalk owns 20% of the company.*

Bill decides to sell 50 shares of his stock to his sister Card. She buys the stock from him for $1.50 per share, which results in Card paying Bill $75. This transaction does not affect the corporation. The corporation still has $500 in cash and 500 shares of stock. Grace still owns 60% of the company, Chalk still owns 20%, and Bill and Card each own 10% of the company. No matter how much stock is sold by the stockholders in the secondary market, or for what price, the corporation will receive no more money. The only way the firm will receive more money is by selling some or all of the 500 shares of stock it still owns.

Just as companies do not issue stock because they want everyone to share in the company's wealth, people do not buy stock because they feel that the company needs help. People purchase a company's stock if they feel they can make money. This money can come in the form of **dividends**, which is paid to the stockholders from the company's profits or money can be made by selling the stock when it rises in price, which is called a "capital gain".

Elaine Pride opens a book store called Bunch of Books with $5,000 she saved. She starts a corporation that owns a total of 10,000 shares of stock, and buys half of it with her $5,000. However, after spending the money necessary to fix up the place, she cannot afford to buy any books. Elaine decides that she needs an additional $5,000 to purchase a selection of books, so she offers people 1% ownership in the store for each $100 that they invest. Russ Howard invests $2,000, which gives him a 20% interest in the book store, Larry Taylor puts in $200 for 2% ownership and Sheila Stamps invests $2,800 for a 28% share in the store.

After a year, Elaine discovers that the book store made a $2,000 profit. She and the three investors decide to put $1,000 of the profit back into the business for expansion and improvements, and divide the other $1,000. The money they decided to split is the "dividends." Since each person gets a portion of the $1,000 equivalent to the amount of ownership that they have in the book store, each receives the following amount:

Elaine	50% ownership	$500
Sheila	28% ownership	$280
Russ	20% ownership	$200
Larry	2% ownership	$20
	================	======
TOTAL	100% ownership	$1,000

Three years later, a book store chain wants to buy Bunch of Books. The chain offers the owners $30,000 for the store. Sheila, Russ, and Larry want to sell the store, but Elaine wants to keep it. They make a deal with the chain whereby the three will sell their shares, and Elaine will sell 1% of her ownership in the business. Elaine agrees to sell 1% of her stock because the only way that the chain will agree to buy the other owners' stock is if they can have more than 50% ownership in the store. Since Elaine has 50%, she must sell 1%, which gives the chain 51% ownership and Elaine 49% ownership. Since the total amount of the offer was $30, 000 and only 51%ownership in the store is being sold, the total amount that the chain actually pays out is $15,300. Each person received the following:

Sheila $8,400 (28%) - $2800 (initial investment) = $5,600 (profit)

Russ $6,000 (20%) - $2000 (initial investment) = $4,000 (profit)

Larry $ 600 (2%)   - $ 200 (initial investment) = $ 400 (profit)

Elaine $ 300 (1%) - $ 100 (initial investment) = $ 200 (profit)

Another reason stock might be issued is to spread the risk of a venture over a number of people, thereby reducing the amount of potential loss that each investor might experience (safety in numbers). By doing so, a greater number of people invest a smaller amount of money. If the project or business does not work, a lot of people would lose a small amount of money instead of a few people losing a lot of money.

Alexis Pride just invented a Check Thin with a reversible pogick. She figures that it will cost about $20,000 to mass produce the product. Although she has $25,000 saved, Alexis knows that there is no guarantee that people will buy the product.

Therefore, she decides to start a company to manufacture the item. The company is called "Buy This Thin."

Before actually manufacturing the product Alexis offers 20,000 shares of stock at a price of $1 per share. This allows her to produce her invention and, by selling some of the stock, reduces the amount she must invest in the company. However, to maintain control of the company, she buys 10,200 shares, which gives her 51% interest in the business.

Since Alexis does not want to go searching for 9,800 people who want to invest $1.00 each, she chooses to sell no less than 100 shares to any individual. Knowing that the most they can lose was $100 and because they feel that a Check Thin with a reversible pogick is just what people need, ninety eight people each buy 100 shares of stock in Buy This Thin.

The previous examples are just two reasons why companies offer stock, and why people buy it. There are many others reasons for buying and selling stock, but that would get much too involved for a book of this kind.

Investment stock is the kind normally offered by companies that have been in existence for many years and have billions of dollars of assets. Most investment stocks can usually be purchased on the major exchanges like the New York Stock Exchange and through the National Association of Securities Dealers Automated Quotation System (NASDAQ).

There are a number of advantages to buying investment stocks. The first one is that many pay dividends. That is, part of the profits from the company is paid out to the stockholders. Some companies allow **dividend reinvestment,** which gives investors the opportunity to use the money that would normally be paid in cash to, instead, be used to purchase additional shares of stock. The second advantage is that investment stocks are often a safer investment than stocks offered by smaller companies. Large companies are typically engaged in many business ventures world wide, which can reduce the possibility of substantial losses, if managed well.

There are also two major disadvantages of purchasing investment stocks. The first is the cost. Most investment stocks range from $10 to $150 or more in price. This means that Grace would have to spend between

$1,000 and $15,000 to buy 100 shares of stock, which is also called a "round lot" of stock. *(While they can and will do so, some brokers do not like handling transactions involving less than 100 shares of stock.)* Obviously, people cannot always afford to buy 100 shares. Another disadvantage of investment stocks, which can also be an advantage, is that its price does not rise very quickly, if at all. This means that the only way of making money is to rely on the dividends from the stock, rather than buying it at one price and then selling it at a higher price within a short period of time.

A Word of Warning

Although I classify large companies as a moderate risk investment, you still must be careful when investing. Normally, the people who run the company receive salaries and bonuses based on the earnings of the company. Also, the price of the stock is affect by the earnings. As a result, people lie and cheat. Two examples of this situation is the Enron Corporation and Global Crossings. Both of those companies knowingly reported false information to the investing public. As a result, many people lost hundreds of millions of dollars. Also, if large companies take very large risks they can also fail. The 2008 bankruptcy of Lehman Brothers, which was a large investment banking company holding $600 billion in assets, is an example of risk taking and reporting false information. Unfortunately, we as small investors have no idea of what goes on inside the companies. We have to resort to the information they report.

INVESTMENT STOCK

ADVANTAGES	
Relatively Safe	Although the economic decline in 2009 has proven that no stock is immune from falling in price, investment stock still represents a relatively safe investment.
Dividends Paid	Investment stocks normally pay dividends on a consistent basis, which means that you get a constant stream of payments for as long as you own the stock.
Dividend Reinvestment	Many large companies allow investors to buy additional shares of stock with their dividends.
Rate of Return	Depending on the stock selected and the price paid, the amount to be made on an investment can be good.
DISADVANTAGES	
Access to Money	While you can sell your stock at any time, there is no guarantee that you can get your money as quickly as you need it.
Brokerage Fees	When you buy and sell stock, the broker you use will charge a fee. This cost, therefore, reduces your gains or increases your losses.
Price Movement	The price of stock normally does not make substantial movements, which means that you cannot rely on price movement to make money in the short term.
Cost to Purchase	Since many of the stocks sell for $10.00 per share or more, buying a block of stock (100 shares) can be considered expensive by some investors.

Corporate Bonds

Bonds are a form of promissory note (I.O.U.) issued by federal, state and local governments, and by corporations that want to borrow large sums of money from the general public. Since the bonds that are issued by the federal, state and local governments were explained in the previous chapter and because they are issued differently than other types of bonds, they will not be discussed in this section.

Unlike babies, bonds do not come from the stork or your fairy godmother. They are also not born in cabbage patches. However, they can make you a lot of lettuce. Bonds come into existence when an agreement called a **bond indenture** is drawn up by the corporation wanting to borrow the money. The bond indenture clearly explains the terms of the loan and the rights and duties of the company borrowing the money. Once the indenture is complete, engraved certificates called **bond certificates** are prepared. Each bond certificate represents a portion of the total amount of money being borrowed by the company. After the certificates have been completed, a bank or trust company is appointed to act as **registrar** and **disbursing agent.** As the disbursing agent, the bank collects all of the interest and principal payments from the borrower and then distributes the money to the people and institutions that purchased the bonds.

When the bonds are ready to be sold, the corporation selling them does not want to spend the time and effort necessary to reach all the little old ladies, little old men and little old children throughout the country. Instead, the total bond issue is normally sold to an investment banking firm, or to a group of investment banking firms known as a **syndicate.** They take over the responsibility of selling the bonds to the little old people.

Bonds fall (especially if you drop them) into two major categories - **zero coupon bonds** and **coupon bonds.** Zero coupon bonds are sold at a price less than the **face** value *(the one printed on the face of the bond)* and at maturity the buyer receives the face value. Zero coupon bonds do not pay any interest before they mature.

Coupon bonds are sold at their face value *(there are exceptions that will be explained later)* and have coupons attached to them. These coupons represent promises to pay specific amounts of interest at specific times. When the time comes to receive an interest payment, a coupon is deposited into the bank and the bank that is functioning as the disbursing agent honors the coupon as if it was a check.

There are five basic types of bonds - mortgage bonds, collateral trust bonds, debenture bonds, convertible bonds and James Bond *(I will only discuss the first four).*

- **Mortgage bonds** use mortgages on real estate as collateral for the repayment of the loan. If the debt is not repaid, the real estate is sold and the proceeds from the sale is used to pay the debt.

- **Collateral trust bonds** use stocks and bonds of other companies, which are owned by the company borrowing the money, as collateral for repayment. If the borrowing company doesn't pay the debt, the sale of the stocks and bonds it owns will cover the payment.

  Mighty Mousetrap Company wants to raise money by issuing bonds. Since the company is new and no one has ever heard of it, few people will be interested in buying its bonds. However, since Mighty Mousetrap owns stock in AT&T, IBM and General Electric, it can issue collateral trust bonds and use the stock as collateral for the repayment of the loan. A bank or trust company can act as trustee and hold the stock. If Mighty Mousetrap cannot repay the loan, the AT&T, IBM and GE stock will be sold by the trustee to repay the debt.

- **Debenture bonds**, which are the most common type of corporate bond, do not have collateral to back them. They are issued based on the credit rating of the firm. As a protection for bond holders, the agreements normally carry provisions that limit the dividends that can be paid to stockholders until the debt from the bonds are paid off. Moreover, if the company declares bankruptcy, the bond holders are considered creditors and will be paid before stockholders receive any money.

- **Convertible bonds** are debenture bonds that allow the holder the right to exchange them for a specific number of shares of stock. This right can either give the bond holder a time limit to make the exchange or the right to make the exchange can exist for the life of the bond.

The amount of interest that Grace can receive from the bonds she buys is based on their rating. Unlike movies, bonds are not rated G, PG, R and X - they are rated AAA to D, and some have no rating. The highest rating that a bond can have is AAA and the lowest have no rating. Ratings from AAA to BBB are considered **investment grade.** This means that bonds within this range are the primary ones that are considered for use in investment portfolios seeking safe investments. Ratings are provided to give potential lenders an idea of the company's credit rating and how well it is run. An action by the company, such as a change in management, can affect the firm's rating. Ratings are given to state, city and corporate bonds. Companies such as Moody's and Standard & Poor's rate the bonds based on the company's financial health. The higher a bond is rated, the safer the investment. The safer the investment, the lower the amount of interest paid by the company.

There are two amounts of money associated with coupon bonds. The first amount is the **face value** of the bond. It is also known as the par value. The face value is the amount that Grace will receive when the bond reaches maturity if she keeps the bond that long. The second amount associated with coupon bonds is the **coupon rate.** The coupon rate represents installment payments that Grace will receive for as long as she keeps the bonds. These installment payments represent interest. The payments are normally made one, two, three or four times a year. Two payments per year *(one every six months)* is the most common.

Throughout the life of the bond, Grace will receive the coupon amount that is stated in the bond indenture. However, when buying a bond there are times when she will have to pay more, less or the same amount of the face value. The cost may vary due to the value of the bond at the time it is purchased. *For those readers who want to get into the nuts and bolts of bond pricing, Appendix B provides a more detailed description.*

Many corporate bonds are **callable,** which means that the companies issuing them have the ability to buy the bonds back from investors before the maturity date. However, investors do not have the ability to turn them back in to the company early. Firms normally **call** the bonds if they can borrow money at a lower interest rate or want to reduce their debt. *(They can also call them if they are lonely.)*

> *The Fred G. Sanford Company is in need of money for expansion. The firm decides to issue bonds that will mature in 10 years, but are callable after 2 years at the par (face) value. Since*

the company's financial health is weak, their bonds have been rated B by the rating companies. The low rating results in the firm having to pay 8% interest to attract investors.

After 3 years, the company becomes more profitable and its rating is upgraded to AA by the rating companies. Since the company is still paying holders of the original bonds 8% interest, they decide to call the bonds and issue new bonds paying 6% interest. Although the investors want to keep their 8% bonds, since the bonds were callable after two years, investors have no choice but to redeem the bonds and receive the face value in cash.

There are two major ways in which Grace can make money with bonds. One way is by simply holding them until the maturity date. This method, which I call "sit on the sofa, watch television and do nothing," involves collecting interest payments every six months during the life of the bonds and then cashing them in for their face value when they mature. With the exception of buying the bonds and collecting her money, this method requires no great involvement or effort on Grace's part.

The other way in which Grace can make money with bonds is by buying them at one price and then selling them at a higher price before they mature. This method requires a greater amount of involvement on her part. Either she or her broker must keep a constant watch on the movement of the bond prices and, if the price does rise or fall, be ready to react quickly. If she does decide to sell her bonds before maturity, until they are actually sold, Grace will still collect interest payments every six months.

CORPORATE BONDS

ADVANTAGES	
Relatively Safe	Depending on a bond's rating, you can feel secure that you will make money and that you will not lose your initial investment.
Small Investment	The amount needed to begin investing is relatively small – approximately $1,000.
Regular Interest Payments	You will receive interest payments on a regular basis for as long as you own the bond.
Rate of Return	The interest rate you receive can be relative good compared to other investments.
DISADVANTAGES	
Access to Money	Since bonds are normally considered long-term instruments, you cannot turn them into cash immediately. While you can usually sell them on the open market, doing so may not occur quickly enough to meet your needs.
Liquidity Risk	If you want to sell the bonds before maturity, you may not be able to receive the same amount that you originally paid.
Callable	You might have to redeem the bonds before they mature, whether you want to or not.

Preferred Stock

What do you get when you cross a common stock with a bond? You get a preferred stock. Like common stock, preferred stock represents ownership in a company. However, like bonds, it is structured with a fixed dividend and normally must be paid before common stock dividends are paid. Unlike common stock, where ownership in a corporation lasts until you sell it, preferred stock often matures at a certain period in time -- typically from 30 to 50 years after it is initially issued. Preferred stock can also be callable, which can result in you having to turn it in for cash.

Preferred stock comes in a number of shapes and sizes. The most common types are described below:

- **Cumulative Preferred Stock** – if one or more dividend payments are not made at the specified time because the company is unwilling or unable to pay, the payments will accumulate and must be paid before common stock dividends are paid.

- **Noncumulative Preferred Stock** – dividends that are not paid do not accumulate, and are gone forever.

- **Participating Preferred Stock** – investors share in any extra profits, over and above the stated dividend, that a company might earn in prosperous years so that they will receive a return that is at least equal to that earned by common stock holders. Additionally, the investors might have some voting rights in determining company affairs.

- **Nonparticipating Preferred Stock** – investors have no voting rights and do not receive any profits other than the stated dividends.

- **Convertible Preferred Stock** – there is normally a provision that the owner may exchange the preferred stock for a certain number of shares of the company's common stock.

Like bonds, preferred stock is rated by organizations such as Standard & Poor's and Moody's. The risk related to preferred stock is based on its credit rating. Therefore, you should consider the company's credit rating and background. As with other investments, you can make money with preferred stock by receiving dividends at the specified periods. Also, you might be able to make money by selling the stock at a price high than you originally paid.

PREFERRED STOCK

ADVANTAGES	
Relatively Safe	Depending on a stock's rating, you can feel secure that you will make money and that you will not lose your initial investment.
Small Investment	The amount needed to begin investing is relatively small.
Continuous Dividend Payments	Depending on the type of stock you buy, you will receive dividend payments every year for as long as you own the instrument.
Rate of Return	The interest rate you receive can be good.
DISADVANTAGES	
Access to Money	While you can sell your stock on the open market, doing so may not occur as quickly as you would like to sell it.
Liquidity Risk	If you want to sell the stock before maturity, you may not be able to receive the same amount that you originally paid.
No Voting Rights	Many preferred stocks do not have the same voting rights as common stock.
Callable	You may have to redeem the stock before they mature, whether you want to or not.

Commercial Paper

Commercial paper, like bonds, are promissory notes (I.O,U,'s) issued by corporations. Also, like zero coupon bonds, they are purchased at a discounted rate and when they mature, the purchaser receives the face value. The major difference between commercial paper and bonds is that commercial paper is a short-term, rather than long-term, investment. It always matures in less than a year and usually matures in six months or less.

Commercial paper is issued by corporations that want to borrow $50,000 or more from the public for a short period of time. This does not mean that one person is expected to buy paper for the total amount of the debt. Many individuals and institutions buy the paper, which spreads the risk over a number of investors. The minimum amount that Grace can invest in a particular corporation's commercial paper depends on what the firm decides to issue. The smallest amount that I have seen available has been $250.

Firms issue commercial paper either because they have problems borrowing money from banks or issuing the paper is just a lot better than borrowing from banks. Commercial paper can be better because the interest rate a company pays investors could be less than what would be paid to a bank. Additionally, the firm has far greater control over how the borrowed money is used. Quite often, when a corporation borrows money from a bank, the firm must leave 20% of the borrowed money with the bank making the loan. The 20% represents a "compensating balance." Companies have no such requirement when they issue commercial paper.

The rate of interest that Grace can receive when buying commercial paper depends on the credit rating of the company selling the paper. A company's credit rating can range from AAA to D, with AAA being the highest rating. The lower the credit rating, the greater the amount of interest she will receive from the company because there is a greater possibility of Grace losing her total investment.

Renee Olive owns a corporation that manufactures thumb tacks (you could say she runs a tacky business). The firm needs a new machine to make more tacks, but doesn't have the $50,000 required to buy one. She is sure that the company will be able to repay the loan in a few months from the increased sale of tacks.

If Renee borrows the money from a bank, she will have to leave 20% ($10,000) of the loan in the bank as a compensating balance, which results in her having only $40,000 to spend for the machine. This means that she would have to borrow more than actually needed to get the full $50,000, which results in her paying more interest. Moreover, if she borrows from the bank, she will have to pay 15% interest on the loan. However, because the bank would be holding a compensating balance, the actual interest rate she would be paying is 18% because she must also pay interest on the $10,000 being held.

Rather than borrowing money from the bank, the company could issue bonds. However, this would probably not be a wise choice because she will be able to repay the money in six months and does not want to have any long term debts. Also, since bonds are normally purchased by people for a long term investment, this would not interest bond buyers.

A third alternative is for the corporation to sell commercial paper. This might be the best alternative because Renee can raise the full $50,000 needed and the interest rate could possibly be lower than what the bank charges. If she pays 12% interest to the buyers of the commercial paper, Renee will be better off because of the lower amount of interest being paid. The lenders will also be better off because they will be receiving a higher rate of return than would be received by investing in some of the other instruments. Additionally, if the company's credit rating is good, it should be relatively easy to sell because the paper will be of interest to people looking for a short-term investment.

Commercial paper is usually sold by very large corporations with good credit ratings. However, companies with poorer credit rating and new companies with no performance track record can hope to induce investors to buy their paper by paying higher interest rates. Additionally, weaker companies might find it better to issue paper in small denominations because it might be easier to sell paper in $250 increments rather than in $1,000 increments.

COMMERCIAL PAPER

ADVANTAGES	
Relatively Safe	Depending on a company's credit rating, Commercial Paper can be a relatively secure investment.
Small Investment	A large amount of money might not be needed to begin investing.
Rate of Return	The interest rate you receive can be good.
DISADVANTAGES	
Access to Your Money	Although Commercial Paper is a short-term investment, you cannot get your money out whenever you wish – you might have to wait until maturity or try to sell it in the secondary markct.

Mutual Funds

Mutual funds have become a major investment vehicle for both individuals and businesses. Trillions of dollars are invested in mutual funds. However, most investors have no idea of how funds work, or why one is a better choice than another. I strongly believe that if you brush your teeth after every meal, floss every day and read this section carefully, you will have a much better understanding about this type of investing.

Mutual funds are financial instruments offered by investment companies. People give their money to these companies and the companies invest the money in various instruments. The kinds of instruments in which a mutual fund invests depend on its investment strategy. The amount of money Grace can make on her investment depends on how well the mutual fund performs. If the investments made by a fund rise in price, the value of her shares will be higher. If they do not perform well, the value will be lower. Since all mutual funds place money in numerous investments, there is a good chance that she will not lose her total investment.

There are two principal types of mutual funds – closed-end funds and open-end funds. Closed-end mutual funds are treated like stock. That is, the fund's shares are offered to the public through an initial public offering. Once they are purchased, the investor cannot sell the shares back to the mutual fund company. Instead, if an investor no longer want the shares, like stock, they must be sold in the secondary market to another investor who want to purchase them. The price can be higher, lower or the same amount paid by the person selling the shares. In 2011, there were more than 600 closed-end funds in the United States with combined assets of almost $250 billion.

Open-end funds are offered by mutual fund companies that are willing to buy back their shares from investors at the end of every business day for the Net Asset Value (NAV). *(Net Asset Value will be explained later in this section.)* Unlike closed-end funds, open-end funds are sold to the public and purchased by from the public by the mutual fund during every business day. In 2011, there were more than 7,500 open-end mutual funds in the United States with combined assets of almost $12 trillion. This section covering mutual funds will focus on open-end mutual funds, but closed-end funds are very similar.

> *Richard Knight feels that he's got the right stuff to be a "hot shot" investor. However, he has one small problem - very little money. To rid himself of this little setback, Richard decides to form an investment corporation called Investments Galore. With Investments Galore, Richard gets people to put money into a pool (not a swimming pool). This way he can take his money, combine it with other investors' money, and buy securities that neither he nor the other people could afford to purchase individually. Also, he will not spend as much in brokerage fees as he would when investing alone. If Richard is right, and the pool makes good investments, the investors will be swimming in money,*

A good reason for Grace to use this method of investing instead of investing in individual items is because the funds can buy and sell stocks, bonds, treasury bills, etc. much cheaper due to the large volume handled at one time. Also if she doesn't have much money to invest or if she prefers to let someone else handle her finances, mutual funds can be more attractive. The lack of time or expertise to invest in financial instruments on their own is another reason people decide to put their money into mutual funds.

Grace has $1,500 that she wants to invest. However, because she is so busy making money, she doesn't have the time to make a lot of investment decisions. Also, since she has not had the time to learn about how various investments work (this book had not been written at the time), Grace feels that it is much better for her to let someone else invest her money.

Grace decides to let Investments Galore do the investing for her. By doing so, she is combining her money with money from other investors. As a result, Grace's $1,500 will be invested in stocks, bonds, commercial paper or other instruments offered by big companies. Had she made those investments on her own, far more money in fees would have been spent, Moreover, if one of the companies in the mutual fund gets into financial trouble, because her money has been invested in numerous companies, there will be no adverse effects.

There are two major types of mutual funds - stock mutual funds and bond mutual funds. **Stock mutual funds** pool money to buy stocks in various companies. **Bond mutual funds** invest in bonds and preferred stock. Just as individuals, banks and corporations have different investment goals and strategies, mutual funds invest in various instruments. Therefore, Grace must decide which would be the best for her goals.

Although people have been investing in mutual funds for many years, most people, including the "financial professionals" have misconceptions about how they actually work. The section below addresses some of those misconceptions.

Mutual Fund Misconception #1

I have found that many people have a misunderstanding about how mutual funds earnings are reported. Quite often, when people with whom I have spoken sees that a mutual fund has increased by 20% or 30% from the previous year, they have the impression that it means they have received 20% or 30% interest on their investment. This is as wrong as wearing a striped tie with a polka-dot suit. First, and foremost, mutual funds do not pay investors interest. The word "interest" implies that you are loaning money to a fund and expect to receive a specified amount back for the loan. People who buy mutual funds are not loaning money to the fund -- they are giving money managers their money to invest. If the managers are successful, money is made. If not, money is lost (the managers get paid either way). The total annual return reported by mutual funds is made up of three elements -- the net asset value of the fund, dividends paid and capital gains earned.

Net Asset Value (NAV) -- The value of one share of a mutual fund is called the Net Asset Value. The NAV is determined by the net assets (all of the cash and securities owned by the fund, minus the expenses) divided by the number of shares owned by investors. If the price of the securities in the mutual fund increases, the NAV will be higher. If the price of the securities in the mutual fund goes down, the NAV will be lower.

Dividends Paid -- Whenever interest or dividends are paid by the stock or bond being held by the fund, they do not go directly to people who invest in the fund -- they go to the fund itself. Then a portion is distributed to the fund shareholders in the form of dividends. Once dividends are paid, investors have the option of either receiving the cash or reinvesting it. If it is reinvested, additional shares of the fund are automatically purchased at the net asset value of the fund at the time of reinvestment or at the public offering price.

Capital Gains Earned -- If a fund sells some of the securities that it owns for a profit, investors will receive a portion of the profits in the form of a capital gain. As with dividends, shareholders normally have the option to receive the cash or reinvest the money.

Dividends and capital gains are two parts of a mutual fund in which an investor realizes an actual return. That is, when dividends or capital gains are distributed, investors can receive money. However, just like with stocks, profits from an increase in the net asset value of a fund are only realized after the shares have been sold. Therefore, if the NAV of a fund at the beginning of the year is $10 per share and it is $13 per share at the end of the year, the fund has increased by 30%. Unless the shares are actually sold, the 30% gain will not be realized. As a result, if a person decides to invest in a particular fund because it increased by 30% the previous year, they could be very disappointed.

Example #1

Marsha Brady manages a growth and income fund called "The Brady Growth and Income Fund." At the beginning of the year, the net asset value of the fund is $10 per share. Marsha's sister Jan owns 100 shares, which means that the total value of her investment is $1,000. In February, some of the stocks in the portfolio increases in value, which causes in the net asset value of a share to increase to $10.50 per share. During that time, the fund sells some to the stock in its portfolio for a profit, which results in a capital gain distribution of 20¢ per share. Since she owns 100 shares of the fund, Jan has earned $20 and has the option of receiving the cash or reinvesting it by buying additional shares of the fund. If she elects to reinvest it, because the net asset value is now $10.50 per share, Jan will receive 1.9 shares of the fund.

During the year, a dividend of 50¢ per share is distributed to each shareholder. Since Jan now owns 101.9 shares of the fund, she will receive $50.95. If she chooses to reinvest the dividends and the net asset value is still $10.50 per share, Jan will receive 4.85 shares, for a total of 106.75 shares of the fund.

At the end of the year, the net asset value is $11.25, which is a 12.5% increase in value. When reporting the annual return on the fund, the following elements are added together:

Capital Gains	*$0.20 per share*
+ Dividends	*$0.50 per share*
+ Net Asset Value	*$11.25 per share*
	————————
Annual Return	*$11.95 per share*

The Brady Growth and Income Fund will report an annual return of 19.5% for the year, which is the difference between the $10 net asset value at the beginning and the $11.95. The value of Jan's investment is now $1,200.94, which represents 106.75 shares at a value of $11.25 per share. However, the actual realized gain for the year is only 7% (70¢). Therefore, she will only pay income taxes based on the $0.70 per share she earned, not on $1.95 per share.

Example #2
Greg Brady manages a growth fund called "The Brady Growth Fund." At the beginning of the year the net asset value of this fund is $10 per share. Greg's brother Peter owns 100 shares of the fund. In August, the fund's net asset value increases to $13 per share. Greg sells a portion of the stock in the portfolio, which results in a capital gain for the investors of 15¢ per share. Peter's 100 shares have earned him $15 and reinvesting it at the current price of $13 per share yields him 1.15 additional shares.

At the end of the year, the fund's net asset value increases to $13.10 per share. When reporting the annual return of the fund, the following elements are combined:

Capital Gains	*$0.15 per share*
+ Net Asset Value	*$13.10 per share*
	————————
Annual Return	*$13.25 per share*

The Brady Growth Fund will report an annual return of 32.5% for the year, but the amount actually earned from the capital gains is only 1.5% (15¢ per share). The actual value of Peter's investment is now $1,325.07, which represents 101.15 shares at a value of $13.10 per share. Therefore, he will only pay income taxes based on the $0.15 per share he earned, not on $3.25 per share.

The two examples illustrate the differences between the fund strategies. While the value of Peter's shares is greater than Jan's, Jan actually earned more shares because the growth and income fund distributed more cash for reinvestment. Although funds have different strategies, they all invest in one or a combination of the three investment categories -- cash, fixed income and equity.

- **Cash Investments** are those things that can be turned into cash quickly, such as Treasury Bills, Commercial Paper and short-term Certificates of Deposit.

- **Fixed Income Investments** are investments with a fixed rate of interest or dividends, such as bonds and preferred stock.

- **Equity Investments** are investments that represent ownership in a business, such as common stock and limited partnership units.

Mutual Fund Misconception #2

Another misconception that exists is that the value of a mutual fund does not go down in value. As I previously stated, when investing with a mutual fund, you are buying the shares, not loaning the fund company money. If the investments made by the fund go down instead of up, your investment will be worth less money.

Mutual Fund Misconception #3

A third major misconception about mutual funds is that you know how much you will receive for the shares at the time you put in a request to sell them. Unlike selling stocks or bonds, mutual fund shares arc not sold while the market is open. You must place the order to sell during the normal market hours. However, after the market closes, the fund calculates that value of the shares of all its current holdings and then redeems your mutual fund shares based on the value calculated. As a result, if the stock or bond market goes down on the day you place your sell order, you might receive less money than expected.

Mutual Fund Misconception #4

A final major misconception about mutual funds is that a bond or fixed income fund will not go down in value very much, if at all. I believe that this opinion comes from the idea that, if you hold a bond until maturity, you will get your initial investment back. Although this is true for many individual fixed income investments, remember that when buying a bond mutual fund, you are not investing in individual bonds. As a result, there is no set maturity date for the mutual fund. Normally, if interest rates begin to rise, the NAV of a bond mutual fund will begin to decline.

In my opinion, a bond mutual fund is one of the worst investments available because when interest rates go up, the bond mutual fund's NAV goes down. This means that if you sell it, you will be doing so at a loss. Conversely, if interest rates go down, the NAV of the fund will go up, but as the fund buys new bonds for the fund, the new bonds' interest rates will be lower, so the investor will be paid a lower dividend. If you are interested in a fixed income investment and you have enough money, it is much better to buy individual bonds instead of investing in a bond mutual fund.

The following represents the types of investments made by mutual fund companies:

- **Diversified common stock funds** are funds that consist primarily of common stocks. The funds can have a variety of investment objectives. One objective might be conservative, and invest primarily in stocks of companies that are large and well established. Another objective might be more aggressive and invest primarily in growth stocks. Other companies might have the objective of investing in a combination of stock of large, medium and small companies.

- **Income funds** often have an investment objective of generating high current income. This type of fund will invest in companies that pay a high dividend relative to their market price.

- **Balanced funds** maintain some proportion of their investments in bonds and preferred stock, and some in common stock. The proportion of bonds and stocks varies based on the condition of the bond and stock markets, but there will always be some kind of balance. Balanced funds tend to show less volatility than common stock funds. Normally they decline less in periods when the market declines and advance less when the market advances.

- **Bond funds** invest solely in bonds and have the objective of generating stable income for the investors. There are a variety of bond funds. Tax-exempt bond funds invest in municipal bonds and attempt to provide a high rate of return with a high degree of security. U.S. government bond funds offer a high degree of stability by investing only in U.S. government securities.

- **Fixed Income funds** invest in both bonds and preferred stock, with the objective of current income and safety of principal.

- **Specialized funds** invest a large proportion of their assets in a particular industry such as the healthcare industry, the computer industry or any other industry. A specialized fund may also have the objective of investing its assets in a particular geographic area such as a particular state or group of states or a foreign country.

Most mutual funds fall into one of two categories - load funds and no-load funds.

- **Load funds** are sold through brokerage firms, banks and other channels. These funds have sales charges based on a percentage of the total amount invested. Fees are also charged for service, custody, management, reports and administration. The sales charge (load) can be charged in one of three ways:

   Front-end Load (A shares) - the sales charge is paid when the fund is initially purchased.

   Back-end Load (B shares) - the sales charge is paid when the fund shares are sold. However, if the shares are held for a set amount of time, no sales charge will be assessed. Management and other internal fees are normally higher than the A shares.

   Level Load (C *or L shares)* - the sales charge is spread over the time in which the fund is held by the buyer. As with B shares, if held for a certain period of time, no sales charge will be assessed. Also, as with B shares, management and internal fee are normally higher than the A shares.

   The type of loaded fund you choose should be based on the length of time that you plan to hold the shares.

- **No-load funds** are purchased directly from the investment company and do not have a sales charge. However, just like the load funds, fees are charged for management and administration. In fact, depending on how long a fund is held, a no-load fund can be more expensive than a load fund.

Grace has the option of investing with a load fund and paying a sales charge or investing with a no-load fund with no sales charge. The reason that she might prefer to pay a sales charge to a fund is because of the extra services she will receive. Load funds can offer extra services such as arranging for her money to be automatically deposited into the fund from her bank account. With load funds, she can open an account and forget about it - everything will be taken care of by the fund. Moreover, if she already has an account with a stockbroker, Grace doesn't have to spend time looking for a fund or examining their investment strategy and the funds will be reported on a brokerage statement with all of her other investments. While she can invest in a fund and forget it, there are times when change a fund is prudent. Grace must decide whether the extra services are worth a percentage of her investment.

Switching Between Funds

Many investment companies offer a wide variety of mutual funds. The group of funds run by an investment company is called a "Fund Family." Often, within one company's fund family, you can buy growth, income or other funds. In fact some companies use many of the same types of investments in their portfolios. Although the same types of funds from different families do not perform exactly the same, they do perform in a similar manner. Therefore, if you are considering changing from one type of fund strategy to another, it is usually better to see if there is a fund in the same fund family that uses the strategy you want. By doing this, if you have a load fund, you normally do not have to pay additional sales charges.

MUTUAL FUNDS

ADVANTAGES	
Relatively Safe	Investments in funds can be safer than individual instruments because of diversification. If some of the fund's investments prove to be bad, others that make money may offset the losses.
Knowledgeable Investors	Having the personnel, research facilities and experience, fund companies are capable of handling all details involved with investing.
Versatility	Since many investment companies run a variety of funds, you often have the ability to move your money into a variety of funds operated by the same company.
Small Investment	Depending on the mutual fund, you can open an account with as little as $50.00.
DISADVANTAGES	
Unknown Investments	It is normally very difficult to know exactly what investments are being made by the fund, or whether the fund is actually making the types of investments that it claims to be making.
Unknown Expenses	Due to the way the funds report earnings, it is extremely difficult for the average person to determine the actual costs passed on to investors.
Unknown Amount Received When Selling	Since your order to sell will not be executed until after the market closes and the share price is recalculated, there is no way of knowing the actual amount you will receive.
Access to Your Money	If you wish to redeem your mutual fund shares for cash, it can take up to a week to receive the funds, which might not be fast enough to meet your needs.

Unit Investment Trusts

Like mutual funds, Unit Investment Trusts (UITs) are established by investment companies for the purpose of investing in a "basket" (group) of securities and investors purchase units (shares) in the trust. Also, like mutual funds, UITs use various types of investment strategies. However, there are a number of major differences between a mutual funds and a UIT.

- **Fixed Portfolio** -- unlike mutual funds, where the securities in the portfolio change based on the fund manager's view of the market, the stocks or bonds in a UIT generally remain fixed for the life of the trust, so what you see is what you get.

- **Not Managed** -- because the portfolio is fixed, a UIT is not managed and do not charge an annual management fee. Instead, a sales charge is assessed based on the number of units being bought. The trustee of the UIT handles all record keeping and regular payments, and issues annual reports.

- **Set Time Period** -- unlike many mutual funds that can last for an unlimited amount of time, most UITs last one or two years. After the specified period, investors often have the opportunity to either reinvest their money into another UIT, or receive the value of their investment in cash. The amount received can be more or less than the original investment.

In a Unit Investment Trust, investors have the opportunity to buy units in a portfolio of securities that are developed to meet a stated objective. After the units are initially issued, the value of each unit goes up or down based on the securities in the portfolio. Typically, UITs hold between twelve and fifty securities. While the trust is not actually managed, the portfolio is regularly reviewed to assure the financial viability and/or credit worthiness of the securities. If the investment company believes that it is in the best interest of the investors to sell a security before the UIT ends, it can do so.

Income generated from the investments in a trust is usually paid at regular intervals -- typically monthly for fixed income instruments such as bonds and quarterly and/or annually for stock. When income is paid, the investor has the opportunity to either receive the cash or reinvest it back into the UIT for additional units at the net asset value at the time. Units can be sold at any time without the investor paying a fee or penalty. The money that the investor receives will be based on the net asset value at the time of selling the unit, which means that the money received may be more or less than the original amount invested.

UNIT INVESTMENT TRUSTS

ADVANTAGES	
Relatively Safe	Since UITs normally invest in between twelve and fifty securities, your investment is diversified, which helps to reduce the chance of a major reduction in the value of the units.
Knowledge of Investments	You know exactly what the trust is investing in and, under normal circumstances, the investment portfolio will not be charged.
Small Investment	Depending on the UIT, you can invest as little as $100.
DISADVANTAGES	
Variable Rate of Return	Although you can sell your units at any time, there is no guarantee that the net asset value of the units will be greater than or equal to your original investment.
Access to Your Money	If you wish to redeem your UIT shares for cash, it can take up to a week to receive the funds, which might not be fast enough to meet your needs.

Chapter 4
-- High Risk Investments

High risk investments are the kind in which you cannot only lose all the money you've invested, but in some instances more than you originally invested. With some investments you never know exactly how much you can ultimately lose until it actually happens.

Some people compare most of these types of investments to gambling in Las Vegas. True, there is a big risk involved in both gambling at a crap table and gambling that the price of pigs will rise in six months. However, I don't agree that the same kind of risk is involved because, except from a few winos, you can't get any good technical advice on how to shoot craps. This is not to say that all brokers know any more about commodities than winos know about gambling -- just that most brokers appear to be sober when providing their advice. A commodities broker I once met said that he felt so much stress when investing a client's money (thousands of dollars at a time), every evening when riding the train home, he stood outside between the cars and got sick. The interesting thing was that the speculator, a Texas millionaire, didn't let the losses bother him.

Overnight you can find yourself either very rich or very poor. There are two ways to approach high risk investments. One way is to treat them the same way that Superman treats Kryptonite. That is, stay as far away from them as possible (or keep them locked in a lead container).

The second method of approaching high risk investments is to use only the money you don't need. If you have money you would be willing to flush down the toilet, don't flush - speculate in the market. In most instances, it is very difficult to ignore the possibility of losing $500 or more. However, if you can't face the fact that this can happen, high risk investments are not for you.

Personally, when I put money in a risky investment, I see the venture as being either a great money maker or a good tax deduction. I don't like to lose money any more than the next person. However, I never let it bother me if it happens. I find that many speculators are as happy as a pig in mud when their investment is making money, but starts threatening their broker, kicking their dog and questioning their very existence if the price goes against them. My advice to these people is don't threaten your broker, don't kick your dog, don't question your existence and don't speculate.

Before opening accounts for speculative investments, brokers routinely ask the prospective customer to complete various forms. The forms clearly state that there is a high risk involved with investing in certain instruments and that the investor could lose all of their money. By signing the forms the person is acknowledging that fact. The broker also must get background information on the person to make sure that she can afford to speculate. Most reputable brokerage houses will not allow you to engage in really risky investments unless you meet minimum financial requirements. One might think that the broker is truly trying to look out for his client, which might be partially true. However, the brokerage house is mainly looking out for itself. A broker knows that if the speculator can't afford to speculate, he will constantly be bombarded with telephone calls, threats and name calling when the market moves in the wrong direction. In fact, even people who can afford to speculate will do the same thing. There is also a possibility that the brokerage firm could get sued by the investor.

Speculative Stocks

Speculative stocks do not taste, feel or smell any differently than other stocks traded on the various stock exchanges. If Grace told a broker that she wants to purchase "100 shares of speculative stock," the broker would probably tell her that he can't find a company named "Speculative" on any of the exchanges. He would then suggest that she buy stock in another company. Buying stock in a company that doesn't have a long history of having made money, that does not have a large amount of cash to operate or that isn't run well, is usually considered a speculative purchase. There is always a greater chance that companies in those conditions may go out of business more quickly than financially stable, well run firms. However, a company that is considered a sound investment one day can be speculative the next.

Many speculative stocks are traded on the Over-The-Counter Bulletin Board (OTCBB) and on the OTC Markets (formerly called "Pink Sheets"). These two markets carry stocks not listed on a major exchange such as the New York and NASDAQ. Instead, they are traded through computers and over the telephone through "market makers" who negotiate prices. Price quotations for stocks traded in these two forums are in the form of bid and asked amounts. The **bid** price is the amount offered by people and companies that want to purchase the stock. The **asked** price is the amount for which the current stockholders want to sell their stock. If you are buying the stock, you will pay the asked price. If you are selling the stock, you will receive the bid price. The difference between the two prices is called the **spread**. If the spread is too large, the stock will probably not sell.

As with investment stocks, speculative stocks have advantages and disadvantages. The first advantage is that many are considerably cheaper than investment stocks. It is possible for you to pay as little as $0.001 per share for stock in some companies. The second advantage is that because speculative stocks are usually much cheaper than investment stocks, they are more likely to double or triple in price very fast. A slight upward price movement can result in a great amount of money being made.

Grace has $600 to spend in the stock market, excluding the broker's fees. With her money, she decides to use $300 to buy speculative stocks and $300 to buy investment stocks. The speculative stock that Grace buys is in a company called Podunk Plumper. Since stock in the company sells for $0.30 per share, her $300 yields her 1,000 shares. With the other $300, Grace buys stock in AT&T, which costs $30 per share. She has enough money to buy only 100 shares of AT&T stock.

One month later, both the Podunk Plumper and the AT&T stock have increased by $0.30 per share. The Plumper stock is now selling for $0.60 per share, which is a 100% rise in price. The AT&T stock is selling for $30.30 per share, which is a 1% rise in price. Since Grace owns 1,000 shares of Podunk Plumper, she has made $300. The 100 shares of AT&T stock earn her $30.

Although making money buying speculative stocks seems relatively easy, there are some disadvantages to speculating. One disadvantage is that most of the companies selling the stock pay no dividend. Either the companies have no profits or all the profits are reinvested back into the company to make it grow. As a result, the only way to make money on speculative stocks in the short term is to hope that the price rises and then sell it at a profit. The previous example has shown that this strategy could be very good, but there is a second disadvantage - the stock prices can go down just as quickly and easily as they can rise. Moreover, just because the price of one share of stock is $0.01, don't think that it can't go down in price. I personally know of companies with stock prices of $0.003 and less.

> *Grace currently owns 1,000 shares of Podunk Plumper stock that is selling for $0.30 per share and 100 shares of AT&T stock that is selling for $30 per share. After two months, the prices of both the Podunk Plumper and the AT&T stock fall $0.15 per share. The Plumper stock is $0.15 per share, which is a 50% decline in price. The AT&T stock is $29.85 per share, which is a ½% decline in price. Since Grace owns 1,000 shares of Podunk Plumper, she has lost $150. With the 100 shares of AT&T stock she loses $15.*

Speculative stocks costing less than $5 are commonly referred to as "penny" stocks. Since their prices are so low, you can buy a lot of shares for a small amount of money. You can also impress your family and amaze your friends by telling them that you own 20,000 shares of stock in a company. Of course, if you want to impress them, don't mention that, at $0.01 a share, you only paid $200 for the stock. Moreover, don't think that owning 20,000 shares of penny stock means that you own a large portion of the company. You will usually find that when stock is that low in price, millions of shares have been issued. Also, be very careful when selecting penny stocks, especially those that are listed only on the OTC Markets. Companies that are listed on the national stock exchanges and on the OTCBB are required to file quarterly and annual financial statements. Companies only listed on the OTC Markets are not. If a company does not file their financial statements, there is absolutely no way of knowing anything about the company's financial health, what they are doing or any other issues that you should know before buying the shares.

SPECULATIVE STOCK

ADVANTAGES	
Low Investment	Prices per share can begin extremely low, which allows you to buy a lot of shares for a relatively small amount of money.
Earning Potential	The price of stocks can make substantial movements, which is the only way people can make money.
DISADVANTAGES	
Access to Your Money	There is no guarantee that you will be able to sell your stock. Also, if you do sell it, there is no guarantee that you can get your money as quickly as you might need it.
No Dividends	Speculative stocks normally do not pay a dividend, which means that you must rely on an increase in a stock's price to make money.
Risk	A great deal of risk exists with investing in these stocks because either the company or their line of business does not have a proven track record.
Limited Information About the Company	Many companies traded solely on the OTC Markets do not file any financial information, which means that you do not know what is happening internally.
Loss Potential	The price of stocks can make substantial movements downward. You could lose your total investment.

Commodities

The primary difference between a stock and a commodity is that stock is spelled "s-t-o-c-k" and commodity is spelled "c-o-m-m-o-d-i-t-y." There are other differences as well. When you buy or sell stock, you are actually buying or selling part ownership in a corporation. However, when you buy or sell a commodity, you are buying or selling actual products like eggs, cattle, corn or gold.

A commodity agreement (called a **contract)** comes into existence when one party agrees to buy and another agrees to sell a certain item on a specified date. However, as with stocks and other financial instruments, the buyer does not know from whom he is buying and the seller does not know to whom she is selling *(nor does either really care).*

Three kinds of commodities markets are in existence - a **spot** market, a **forward** market and a **futures** market. On a much smaller scale, when you buy eggs at the supermarket you are actually buying in the spot market. That is, buying in the spot market means that you give someone money and immediately take possession of the product. You pay whatever the price happens to be at the "moment" of the transaction. I emphasize the word "moment" because, while the price of eggs does not change from minute to minute in the supermarket, they can do just that in the other markets. The price changes can either be in your favor or against you. In fact, from the time that your broker tells you that the price of cocoa is $10, you tell him to sell and he places the order, cocoa could have had numerous price changes and you might not be able to sell it at the quoted price. The forward and futures markets work differently than the spot market.

In May, Grace hears about a new car called the Porcupine that is coming on the market in December. She decides that she wants to be the first one to own a Porcupine, so she rushes down to the dealer and tells the salesman that she wants to buy the car. Since the salesman knows that the car will cost $5,000 and he doesn't want to lose the sale, he draws up a contract stating that the dealership is selling Grace the car for $5,000 and it will be delivered in December. To consummate the deal, Grace gives the salesman a $500 deposit.

When the time comes to pick up the car in December, Grace must pay the dealer $4,500. Even if, when the car becomes available, it costs $4,000 instead of $5,000, by signing a contract Grace has made a commitment to pay $5,000. In contrast, if when the car is actually introduced in December its costs $8,000, Grace will only have to pay $5,000 because of the signed agreement.

Just like the car for which the order was placed had not been built when the deposit was paid, when you buy corn, wheat or any forward or futures contract, the products are nonexistent when they are being purchased. The forward and the futures markets are similar in the sense that you buy products that will be delivered at a later date. However, there are a few key differences. In the forward market, products can be bought and sold in any agreed on quantity or quality and delivered at any agreed on place. Furthermore, buyers and sellers do not have to be licensed by any type of exchange.

> *Larry Fine wants to buy 1,000 bushels of corn. He contacts Moe Howard, a local farmer, about purchasing Moe's corn. They enter into an agreement whereby Larry will buy the corn and it will be delivered to Larry's cousin Curley's factory six months later. Since this is the first time that they are doing business together, Moe requests a 50% deposit.*

The previous example illustrates how the forward market works. The commodity futures market, while still involving buying products for future delivery, does not operate in the same manner. Futures trading can only be done on commodities exchange and conducted through licensed brokers. Each commodity futures contract represents a specific product such as corn, eggs, pork, cocoa, gold, silver, etc. All products are bought and sold in fixed quantities, such as 5,000 bushels of corn; 22,500 dozen eggs; 38,000 pounds of pork bellies or 100 ounces of gold. Additionally, each type of commodity has a set date when it must be delivered and the balance paid, and a set location where it must be delivered. No exceptions can be made.

You may wonder why in the name of the Sugar Plum Fairy would Grace want to buy 38,000 pounds of pork bellies when her freezer is already half full, or why she would want to sell 5,000 bushels of wheat when she doesn't even have a loaf of bread in the house. The reason is because if she handles things properly, she never has to actually pick up the pork bellies or deliver the wheat. The majority of commodity trading is done in the futures market because most traders are either not interested in actually owning the products or don't actually have them to sell, which is the case when trading is done in the spot and forward markets. To avoid taking delivery of the product if buying it or delivering the product if selling it, the speculator sells or buys an offsetting contract.

People who initially *sell* contracts usually *buy* the same type of contract to relieve themselves of their obligation to deliver a commodity. Conversely, people who initially *buy* contracts typically *sell* the same kind to relieve themselves of their obligation to take delivery of the commodity. In fact, there would probably not be enough products available if everyone who bought a product during the life of a contract actually decided to take delivery.

In the previous example, Grace deposited $500 with a car dealership in May so she could buy a Porcupine automobile for $5,000 in December. The terms of the contract stated that she must take delivery of the car in December and pay the remaining $4,500 no matter how much the same model actually costs at that time.

Prior to the December delivery date, Grace decides that, instead of the Porcupine, she wants a Walrus - an even newer car. She realizes that, because of her contract with the dealership, she is obligated to buy the Porcupine. Grace remembers that her friend Truman said that he wanted to buy a Porcupine, but couldn't afford one since the price has risen to $7,000. She makes a deal with Truman to sell him the Porcupine for $6,000. They agree that Truman will pay her $1,500 in cash for her contract with the dealership. Then, when the December delivery date comes around, he will pay the remaining $4,500 to the dealership and take delivery of the car.

Grace is as happy as a hungry alligator in a YMCA swimming pool because she can now buy the Walrus, made an extra $1,000 and do not have to take delivery of the Porcupine. Truman is as happy as a three-legged lion is a snail race because he has bought the car of his dreams for $1,000 less than he would have had to pay at the dealership.

Another reason that most trading is performed in the futures market is because of the margins. When buying a commodities contract, Grace doesn't have to pay the total amount of the contract at that time. Instead, she pays a **margin,** which is a small percentage of the total cost of the commodity. The margin represents a "good faith" deposit paid by the purchaser to the seller, just like in the earlier example when she gave the car dealer a $500 down payment. For a few hundred dollars, she can control thousands of dollars worth of gold, silver or cocoa.

There are two types of traders in the commodity futures world – hedgers and speculators. **Hedgers** are producers and users of commodities. They actually use or sell the products as a part of their businesses. Hedgers who sell commodities, such as farmers, use the futures market as a way of guaranteeing how much they will be paid for their products. Therefore, no matter how far corn or eggs fall, the hedgers know that they will receive the price stated in the futures contract.

Farmer N. T. Dale grows corn on his farm. At the time he began planting his corn crop; corn was selling for $3.00 a bushel. Since that time, corn has been dropping faster than a prize bull in quicksand and is now selling for $2.50 a bushel. Farmer Dale is concerned. "Holy ham hocks," he replies. "If the corn falls any further I will be ruined! What should I do? What should I do?" Suddenly, he remembers that he can hedge in the commodities market.

Since his corn will be ready for the market in May, Farmer Dale sells a May corn futures contract at the $2.50 price. Selling the contract means that, no matter how much corn will be selling for at harvest time Farmer Dale is guaranteed $2.50 per bushel for his crop.

In the previous example, Farmer Dale appeared to be in great shape if corn prices fall, but would be losing money if the price rises. Actually, he is in good shape in either situation, and he doesn't have to worry about delivering the crop to the place specified by the futures contract.

In May the price of corn has fallen to $1.75 per bushel. Farmer Dale buys a May corn futures contract at the $1.75 price and sells his corn for $1.75 per bushel. Since he previously sold a corn futures contract for $2.50, he makes the $2.50 per bushel price he wanted.

Corn futures contract he originally sold	*$2.50*
Corn futures contract he purchased	*- ($1.75)*

Profit earned from commodities contract	*$0.75*

Amount earned from selling his corn	*+ $1.75*
	=======
Total revenue received	*$2.50*

In May the price of corn has risen to $3.00 per bushel, Farmer Dale __buys__ a May corn futures contract at the $3.00 price, and sells his corn for $3.00. Since he previously sold a corn futures contract for $2.50, he still makes the $2.50 per bushel price he wanted.

Corn futures contract he originally sold	*$2.50*
Corn futures contract he purchased	*- ($3.00)*

Amount lost from commodities contract	*($0.50)*

Amount earned from selling his corn	*+ $3.00*
	======
Total revenue received	*$2.50*

In the second scenario, farmer Dale did not make as much money as he could have made if he had not sold the futures contract and had waited for the price to rise. However, by selling the futures contract, he was able to get the price he wanted, without taking a risk.

Hedgers who buy commodities, such as food processors like Campbells and Kelloggs, use the futures market as a way of guaranteeing how much they will have to pay for the products they buy. Therefore, no matter how high soybeans or wheat rise by the delivery date, the hedgers will only have to pay the amount stated in the contract.

Nellie Bell owns a chocolate factory. One of the main ingredients in producing the chocolate is sugar. Since her largest orders begin right after the Thanksgiving holiday, Nellie purchases her largest quantity of sugar in November. Since she buys sugar on the open market, Nellie is never certain how much she must spend for sugar. The price she pays directly affects the company's profit.

"Heck," replied Nellie. "I sure would like to be guaranteed a set price for this cotton picking sugar so I can determine my expenses and figure out what to charge for my candy." Nellie went on to say "...I know what I can do. I know what I can do! I will buy some of them sugar futures." She purchases a futures contract for 11¢ per pound.

In November, if the price of sugar rises to 12¢ per pound. Nellie can sell an offsetting futures contract. Then, she can buy the sugar in the spot market for 12¢ per pound. The following will result:

Sugar futures contract she originally purchased	*($0.11)*
Sugar futures contract she sold	*+ $0.12*

Amount per pound earned from contract	*$0.01*

Price per pound of sugar purchased	*- ($0.12)*
	======
Total per pound price paid for sugar	*($0.11)*

If the price of sugar declines to 10¢ per pound in November, Nellie can sell an offsetting futures contract. After selling the contract, she can buy sugar in the spot market for 10¢ per pound.

Sugar futures contract she originally purchased	*($0.11)*
Sugar futures contract she sold	*+ $0.10*

Amount per pound lost from contract	*($0.01)*

Price per pound of sugar purchased	*- ($0.10)*
	======
Total per pound price paid for sugar	*($0.11)*

The previous examples illustrate how hedgers, by using the futures market, can determine the amount they will pay for a product. True, Nellie could have paid less for her sugar if the price declined, but she could have also paid a lot more had it increased. No one, except for the psychics who write for the *National Enquirer* or *Star*, knows what will happen in the future.

Speculators are traders who do not actually use the commodities they buy and do not own the commodities they sell. They buy and sell them hoping to make a profit on the price movements. As a futures speculator, Grace must determine whether the price of a commodity will rise or fall. If she thinks it will rise in price, she can make money by buying a contract now and then selling the same kind of contract after the price rises, but before the delivery date arrives.

On June 7, 2000, a palm reader tells you that the price of pork bellies will rise within a year's time. You decide to buy a contract with a delivery date of May 2001. Once you buy the contract, you have until May 2001 to sell a pork bellies contract with the same delivery date (May 2001). If you fail to do this, you should begin clearing out your freezer and be prepared to eat a lot of bacon. If the price of the bellies rises before the delivery date, you can sell your contract and make money. Should your bellies fall and not rise before the delivery date, you still need to sell an offsetting contract to close out your position, but you should also probably go to a different palm reader because you will have lost money.

If, on the other hand, Grace thinks that a commodity will fall in price, she can make money by selling a contract now and buying the same type before the delivery date.

On July 15, 2000, you open your refrigerator and your loaf of bread falls to the floor. To you, this is an omen telling you that the price of wheat will fall sometime this year, so you sell a wheat contract with a delivery date of January 2001. By selling the contract, you will be paid a margin, which is placed in an account. To avoid having to deliver 5,000 bushels of wheat, you must buy a wheat contract with the January 2001 delivery date. If the price of wheat falls (like the bread in the refrigerator), you can buy a contract for less than you sold one, thereby making a profit. Should the wheat rise, you must still buy a contract to avoid having to buy and deliver the wheat, but you will lose money – the difference between the price you received by selling the first contract and the price you paid to buy the offsetting contract. If you fail to buy the wheat contract before the delivery date, you will have to purchase 5,000 bushels of wheat on the spot market and then make delivery to fulfill the contract.

Unlike stocks, where prices can rise or fall to any level in one day, commodity futures contracts have minimum and maximum daily price limits. In the futures market each commodity can only rise within a set range each day. Once the price gets to the limit, trading stops.

The futures market opens on Monday and corn with a May delivery date is trading for $2.81 per bushel. By the time the *market closes on Monday the cost of the corn can't increase to more than $2.91 or fall to more than $2.71. If it closed at $2.91 on Monday, when the market opens on Tuesday a new starting point is set and the corn can't go above the $3.01 limit or below the $2.81 limit.*

Daily limits are set primarily to limit the financial risk to the futures clearinghouse. All transactions are handled through brokers who are members of the clearinghouse. This reduces the chance of impropriety between brokers occurring. Each day after the market closes the members must settle with each other by paying or receiving money to cover changes in contract prices.

Since most futures have not been grown or mined when you enter into the contract, it is impossible to give specific reasons why prices rise and fall. However, things such as weather, politics, war or actions by central banks can affect prices.

COMMODITY FUTURES

ADVANTAGES	
Buying Commodities	
Profit Potential	While there are daily limits on how high or low prices can move, the amount of money you can make by selling commodities is unlimited.
Small Investment	Since you deposit only a small percentage of the total cost of commodity futures, you control large contracts with a small amount of money.
Daily Price Limit	If prices move against you, because of the daily limits, you have a chance of getting out of the market.
Selling Commodities	
Profit Potential	While there are daily limits on how high or low prices can move, the amount of money you can make by selling commodities is unlimited.
Daily Price Limit	If prices move against you, because of the daily limits, you have a chance of getting out of the market.

DISADVANTAGES	
Buying Commodities	
Loss Potential	There is a chance that you could not only lose your total investment, but also be liable for paying out more money.
Time Limitation	You have a limited amount of time to hold a futures contract. If you hold it until it expires, you must take delivery of the product and pay the balance of the money due.
Daily Price Limit	There are limits on how high or low prices can rise and fall. If they move against you to the limit, trading could totally stop, which would result in you not being able to get out of the market to reduce your loss.
Selling Commodities	
Loss Potential	The amount of money you can lose is unlimited since you could be required to sell a commodity that you do not own for far less than its value.
Daily Price Limit	There are limits on how high or low prices can rise and fall. If they move against you to the limit, trading could stop for the day, which would result in you not being able to get out of the market to reduce your loss.
Time Limitation	You have a limited amount of time to hold a futures contract. If you hold it until it expires, you must deliver the product.

If you are a risk taker and decide to venture into the world of commodity futures trading, where fortunes are made and lost with a drop of rain, remember three things if nothing else:

- **You can lose your entire investment.** You should never use money that you can't afford to lose. Commodity brokers are supposed to tell this to potential speculators of the risk. However, regardless of how much people acknowledge this fact, many panic when prices move in the wrong direction. In some cases, this has caused the breakup of homes, marriages and life-long friendships.

- **To thine own self, be true.** If you guessed wrong on a commodity's move, there is no need to panic, but get out. There is no reason to let the rest of your money stay in the investment if you feel that you made an error. As previously mentioned, when buying a contract you have to deposit a certain amount of money in an account. If the commodity's price goes below a certain amount, there will be a **margin call**, which means that if you want to keep the contract, more money must be deposited with the broker. If no deposit is made, the broker will automatically buy an offsetting contract. Since commodity prices can rise as quickly as they can fall, the only time you should meet a margin call is if you know what is causing the price movement and that the price will go your way before the delivery date.

- **Always keep the delivery date in mind.** If you wait too long before buying or selling an offsetting contract, you might wake up one morning to discover that you are the proud owner of a certificate entitling you to 20,000 pounds of live cattle residing somewhere in the Midwest. In their quest to make one more dollar, some traders wait until the last minute before making an offsetting trade. Sometimes this tactic works, but other times they can unintentionally get into the cattle business.

Stock Options

Options can best be compared to an automobile insurance policy. With such a policy, you give an insurance company a certain amount of money, which guarantees that if you have an accident within a specified time, the company will pay for the damages. If nothing happens within that time period or if you do have an accident and decide not to report it, the policy simply runs out. If an auto accident does occur during the time you are insured and is reported, the insurance company is obligated to pay for the damages. Once the policy has expired you then have the option of buying another one with the same stipulations.

Stock options offer the same alternatives as insurance, but in a much broader way. Rather than guaranteeing to pay for damages, an option guarantees that Grace will be able to either buy a certain stock at a specified price (a **Call option)** or sell a certain stock at a specified price (a **Put option)** up to the expiration date of the option. As in the insurance business, if she does not exercise the option before the expiration date, which means that she does not buy or sell the stock, it will simply cease to exist. If Grace decides to exercise the option, thereby electing to buy or sell the stock, none of the money she spends on the option goes toward the stock's purchase price.

Although buying options gives her the right to buy or sell stock at specified prices, there is no real connection between the underlying stock and the option. However, the price of the underlying stock does affect the price of the option. This will be explained in detail a bit later.

In addition to assuming the role of insurance buyer, the options market offers Grace the opportunity of being an options seller. By selling a Call option, she is guaranteeing the option buyer that she will sell them the underlying stock at an agreed on price (called the **strike price).** Grace can also sell a Put option. By doing so, she is guaranteeing the option buyer that she will buy the underlying stock from them at an agreed on price.

While there are both buyers and sellers of options, no particular buyer or seller is directly associated.

> *On Thursday, July 5, at 1:00 p.m., Robert Stein buys a Call option that grants him the right to buy General Electric stock at $20 per share. On Thursday, July 5, at 1:00 p.m., Joe Louis sells a Call option, thereby guaranteeing to sell someone General Electric stock at $20 per share. If Robert elects to exercise his option, Joe could be notified that he must sell his GE stock, but if that happened, it would be purely coincidental. Anyone who has sold the same kind of Call option that Robert bought could be contacted. The system is similar to a lottery.*

Buying Options

There are two kinds of options - Puts and Calls. Buying a Put option gives Grace the right to sell a specific stock at the strike price any time before the expiration date. She should buy a Put option if she feels that the underlying stock will go down in price.

> *In July, Bill Board has a gut feeling that AT&T stock will go down in price by December. Although he doesn't own stock in the company, he decides to buy a Put option for 5½ ($550), with a $65 strike price and has a December expiration date. The stock currently sells for $68 per share. Bill's guts turned out to be right because the stock's price drops to $50 per share. Even though the stock now sells for $50, Bill's Put option guarantees him the right to sell the AT&T stock for $65 per share. Since he doesn't own AT&T shares, Bill can make money by either selling the same type of option (a December AT&T Put Option with a $65 strike price) for a price higher than he paid, or by buying the stock at $50 per share, and immediately exercising his option to sell the stock at $65 per share. By deciding to do the latter of the two things, he will make $950 minus the broker's fee ($1,500 profit from selling the stock minus the $550 price of the option). Had the stock's price not declined, Bill might have been able to sell the option at a lost or it would have expired and he would have a $550 tax deduction.*

Purchasing a Call option gives Grace the right to buy the underlying stock at the strike price at any time before the expiration date. She should buy a Call option if she feels that the underlying stock will rise in price.

> *In May, Dag Wood read that IBM was introducing a new computer. He decided that the stock would go up within the year, so he buys a Call option for 8 ($800), with a $90 strike price and a November expiration date. The stock was selling for $87 per share at the time. Dag was wrong. The stock actually began falling and by November it was down to $80 per share. Since the Call's strike price was $90, if it was exercised, Dag would be paying $10 more for the stock than the current price (which isn't very smart on any planet). As a result of the wrong guess. Dag has an $800 tax deduction.*

> *Had Dag been right, and the stock had risen to $100 per share, the Call would have been more valuable. He could have purchased stock worth $100 per share for $90, which would have resulted in a seller of that type of Call having to sell him IBM stock for a price $10 per share less than its value. If Dag*

*could not afford to buy the stock, which would have been a total
of $100,000, he could probably sell the Call for more than he
paid and still make money.*

Selling Options

In addition to buying options, Grace can sell them. As an options seller,
which is called an options "writer" in financial parlance, she can offer
both Put and Call options. When selling Puts, she obligates herself to
buying the underlying stock at the strike price if the option is exercised.
Grace can sell Puts if she feels that the underlying stock's price will go
up. If it goes up, buyers of the options will normally not exercise them
since they were bought because the buyer expected the stock price to go
down. If the stock does decline, she must be prepared to buy the stock or
she must buy an offsetting Put to relieve herself of the obligation. Once
she receives an exercise notice, there is no way of getting out of buying
the stock. If Grace wants to write Puts, she must maintain a margin
account with her broker so she will be able to pay for the stock if she has
to buy it.

Selling Calls obligates her to selling the underlying stock at the strike
price to the person who exercises their option. Grace can sell Calls if she
feels that the stock's price will fall. Since a fall in the stock's price means
anyone exercising the option will be buying the stock for more than its
worth, the option will probably expire unexercised. However, a rise in
the stock's price will be good for the option buyer and bad for Grace.
Calls can be written whether she owns the stock or not. If she doesn't
own the stock, a margin (deposit) must be placed with her broker to
make sure that she will be able to deliver the stock if it is called.

Options Alternatives and Potential Results

The following provides an overview of the basic options alternatives and the results based on the price movement of the underlying stock.

OPTIONS CHOICES

IF YOU:	THEN YOU:	IF STOCK PRICE GOES UP:	IF STOCK PRICE GOES DOWN:
BUY a CALL OPTION	PAY a PREMIUM (Money)	You MAKE MONEY	You LOSE MONEY
BUY a PUT OPTION	PAY a PREMIUM (Money)	You LOSE MONEY	You MAKE MONEY
SELL a CALL OPTION	RECEIVE a PREMIUM (Money)	You LOSE MONEY	You MAKE MONEY
SELL a PUT OPTION	RECEIVE a PREMIUM (Money)	You MAKE MONEY	You LOSE MONEY

POTENTIAL GAIN OR LOSS

IF YOU:	YOUR MAXIMUM POTENTIAL GAIN IS:	YOUR MAXIMUM POTENTIAL LOSS IS:
BUY a CALL OPTION	UNLIMITED	COST OF YOUR ORIGINAL INVESTMENT
BUY a PUT OPTION	UNLIMITED	COST OF YOUR ORIGINAL INVESTMENT
SELL a CALL OPTION	ORIGINAL CASH YOU RECEIVE	UNLIMITED*
SELL a PUT OPTION	ORIGINAL CASH YOU RECEIVE	UNLIMITED**

*   If you sell a Call option, but don't own the underlying stock, your potential loss is unlimited. If the option is exercised, you must buy the stock at the current price and then sell it to the person exercising the option for the strike price.

**   If you sell a Put option, your potential loss is unlimited because if the option is exercised, you are obligated to buy the underlying stock for the strike price even if the stock is worthless in the open market.

Very, Very Basis Options Strategies

Options are unique in the since that there are a number of ways of playing the market and making money.

As An Options Buyer

You think a stock's price is going down. If you believe that a stock will decline in price, you can buy a Put option. When the price declines you can either sell the option, which will be more valuable, or buy the stock at the lower price and then exercise your option to sell the stock at the strike price, which will be higher.

You think a stock's price is going up. If you believe that a stock will rise in price, you can buy a Call option. When the price rises you can either sell the option, which will be more valuable, or exercise your option to buy the stock at the strike price and then sell it at the higher price.

You know the stock is going up or down in price, but don't know which way. If you are certain that a stock is going to move, but not sure whether it is going to rise or fall, you can buy a Put and a Call option. If the stock goes down you can follow one of the strategies described in the first example with your Put, and try to sell your Call, which may be a problem since the stock moved against it. Conversely, if the stock moves up you can follow one of the strategies described in the second example with your Call and try selling your Put.

As An Options Seller

You think a stock's price is going down. If you believe that a stock will decline in price, you can sell a Call option. If the price of the stock does fall, buyers holding the options will probably not exercise them since they would be paying more for the stock than the current value. When the option expires, you will have made the money you received from the premium.

You think a stock's price is going up. If you believe that a stock will rise in price, you can sell a Put option. If the price of the stock rises, buyers of the Put options will probably not exercise them since they would be selling their stock for less than the current value. When the option expires, you will have made the money you received from the premium.

Although I have offered ways of using Put and Call options for increasing your wealth, as previously stated, **this is not a book on strategy.** If you and interested in playing the options market, first invest in a book that goes more deeply into options. There are other, more complex strategies as well that are well beyond the scope of this book.

STOCK OPTIONS

ADVANTAGES	
Buying Options	
Limited Loss Potential	Although you can lose your total investment, you know exactly how much is at risk.
Unlimited Profit Potential	The amount of money you can make is unlimited since you can either sell the option or buy the stock and then sell it.
Small Investment	The price controls a block (100 shares) of the underlying stock, which is much cheaper than buying the actual stock.
Selling Options	
Fixed Profit Potential	While the amount you can make is limited, if the option is not exercised, you know that you will make money as well as the amount you will make.
Limited Time of Exposure	Since buyers have a limited amount of time to exercise their option, you are only at risk for a limited period of time.
DISADVANTAGES	
Buying Options	
Time Limitation	You have a limited amount of time to hold an option. If it expires before you exercise it, you lose your total investment.
Access to Your Money	You may not be able to sell and offsetting option to reduce your loss or take your profit.
Exercising Expense	If you decide to exercise an option, none of the money spent for the option is applied toward the stock's purchase price.
Selling Options	
Unlimited Loss Potential	The amount of money you can lose is unlimited since you could be required to buy stock for much more than it is worth or sell stock for far less than its value.
Access to Your Money	You may not be able to buy an offsetting option to reduce your loss or take your profit.

Although this section on options discussed stock options, you should be aware that other type of options also exists, which include the following:

- **Options on Foreign Currency**
- **Options on Government Instruments**
- **Options on Agricultural Futures**
- **Options on Metal Futures**
- **Options on Stock Indexes**

Foreign Currency

Trading foreign currency is similar to trading commodities in some ways and different in others. The main similarity is that they both have spot, forward and futures markets. Going to a bank or currency exchange, giving the teller U.S. dollars and immediately receiving Japanese yen is an example of buying currency in the spot market. Entering into an agreement with a company to exchange dollars for Swiss francs at a future date is a forward transaction. Entering into an agreement to buy or sell a standardized amount of a foreign currency, with a standardized expiration date, on an organized exchange is a futures transaction. Another similarity between trading commodities and foreign currency is that you can buy them and never take possession or sell them regardless of whether you actually own them. In fact, unless someone makes a major mistake, a currency buyer in the futures market never actually takes delivery of the currency and a currency seller in the futures market never has to actually deliver it. The major difference between the two activities is that rather than trading things such as pork bellies, eggs and copper, you trade British pounds, Swiss francs and Japanese yen.

As a speculator in foreign currency, Grace must determine whether the U.S. dollar will rise or fall in relation to other currencies in the world.

If Grace has a feeling that the Euro will go down in price, which means that $1 will buy more Euro than it currently does, she can sell a contract in that currency. If she sells a contract when 1 euro costs $1.80 and two months later 1 euro is selling for $1.50, she should rejoice because she has made money. That is, if she sells 100 euro at $1.80 each. It would cost her $30 less to buy back 100 euro. If, however, the euro rises to $2.33 each, she will have lost money since those same 100 euro will cost $53 more to buy than she originally paid. Conversely, if she feels that the euro will go up in price. Grace can buy a contract in that *currency. Then, if it does rise she can rejoice and if it goes down she can weep. Whether the price moves in her favor or against her, Grace must purchase an offsetting contract to avoid having to deliver or take possession of the euro.*

Understanding the ins and outs of foreign currency can be a bit tricky because there are actually two markets - the **Foreign Exchange market** and the **Futures market.** The futures market will be the main topic of this section because a much smaller amount of money is needed to play. However, since the Foreign Exchange market does exist and is available for speculation, it should be discussed.

Foreign Exchange Market

One of the primary functions of the foreign exchange market is to act as an intermediary between buyers and sellers. If Grace wants to buy currency from a country other than the U.S., she can either call throughout the world looking for a seller or buy the currency in the Foreign Exchange market. In the United States, currency prices are always quoted in terms of U.S. dollars. That is, if the British pound closes at $1.25, she must pay $1.25 for each pound. It should be noted that many international airports in the U.S. have currency exchanges that buy and sell small amounts of currency.

Three types of transactions normally occur on the Foreign Exchange market. They are *forward, swap* and *spot* transactions. A **forward** transaction involves buying or selling currencies with a delivery date anywhere from three days to five years in the future - the majority of these transactions mature in one year or less. This type of transaction is most like the futures market.

A **spot** transaction involves trading currency for immediate delivery. The prices on the spot market constantly change. During the time that the market is open, any price quoted is the rate at that instant. If the decision to buy or sell is made moments later, the price may not be the same. These price changes can be the result of political, economic, monetary or other news announcements. They can also change if an extremely high or low amount of a currency is traded. The currency prices of forwards and swaps are based on prices in the spot market. When people travel to a different country, one of the first things that many do after arriving to a new location is to exchange their money for local currency. This exchange is made on the spot market.

A **swap** transaction occurs when a currency is purchased in the spot market and the same amount is simultaneously sold in the forward market. It also happens when a currency is sold in the spot market and the same amount is simultaneously purchased in the forward market.

A swap would be if Grace buys 1 million Swiss francs on the spot market, which means she takes possession of them immediately, and she simultaneously sells a forward contract for 1 million Swiss francs in the Forward market.

Futures Market

Transactions in the Futures market are similar to forward transactions in the Foreign Exchange market. However, because the Futures market is governed by the U.S. Government, and the Foreign Exchange market isn't, the rules and regulations are quite different.

- **Contract Sizes** - In the Foreign Exchange (FX) market, the sizes of the contracts traded are determined exclusively by the buyers and sellers. That is, if a buyer wants 1 million Swiss francs and someone is willing to sell them that amount, a contract can be written.

  Contract sizes in the futures market have been established, and can't be altered. When Grace buys one Swiss franc future contract, she has automatically bought 125,000 francs. If she wants to buy 1 million francs in the futures market, she must buy eight contracts. Contract sizes are as follows:

- Australian dollar.............................100,000 Australian dollars
- Brazilian reals..............................100,000 Brazilian reals
- British pound ....62,500 British pounds
- Canadian dollar ....100,000 Canadian dollars
- Chinese renminbi.........................1,000,000 Chinese renminbi
- Czechoslovakian koruna ....4,000,000 Czech koruna
- Euro-Currency.............................125,000 euro
- Hungarian forint ....30,000,000 Hungarian forint
- Israeli shekel...............................1,000,000 Israeli shekel
- Japanese yen...............................12,500,000 Japanese yen
- Korean won ....125,000,000 Korean won
- Mexican peso...............................500,000 Mexican pesos
- Polish zloty..................................500,000 Polish zloty
- Russian rubles ....2,500,000 Russian rubles
- South African rands....................500,000 South African rand
- Swiss franc ....125,000 Swiss francs

- **Delivery Dates and Contract Lengths** - As with the
  contract sizes in the Foreign Exchange market, the buyer and
  seller also agree on how long a Forward contract will last
  and when delivery will take place.

  In the futures market, buyers and sellers have no choice of
  delivery dates and contract lengths. All contracts last for a
  period of eighteen months, and expire in March, June,
  September or December. This is not to say that if Grace
  buys a futures contract, she must buy it on the first day of
  trading or hold it for eighteen months. Contracts are bought
  and sold many times prior to the date they mature. These
  rules simply establish the guidelines for the contracts
  themselves. Moreover, the delivery day of the contract
  money is always the third Wednesday of that month.

- **Structure of Transactions** - There is a big difference in the
  way that transactions are handled in the Forward versus the
  Futures markets. A purchase in the Foreign Exchange market
  simply requires that Grace has a sufficient amount of money
  on deposit in a bank to cover the transaction.

  A purchase in the Futures market requires the purchaser of a
  contract to pay the seller a "margin." A margin represents a
  "good faith" deposit and represents a percentage of the total

cost of the contract. The minimum amount that she must deposit is set by the exchanges. It is normally in the 5% range, which means that she only has to deposit $5 for each $100 that the contract represents.

As previously stated, there are similarities between the Forward and Futures markets. The following are some of those similarities:

- **Daily Movements** - Neither the Futures nor the Forward market have daily price limits. This means that the price of a currency can move as high or low as the market dictates. This can be either a blessing or a curse. It all depends on whether Grace buys or sells the contracts.

- **Ownership** - Grace does not have to actually own a foreign currency to sell a Futures or Forward contract, nor must she actually take delivery on a contract she has purchased. The trick is to get in and out of the market before the delivery date arrives.

If Grace buys a British pound contract with a June delivery date, to avoid being loaded with pounds, she must sell a British pound contract with a June delivery date. If she sells a Swiss franc contract with a December delivery date and she doesn't want to have to buy them in order to fulfill the delivery obligation, she simply buys a Swiss franc contract with a December delivery date.

A very small percentage of contracts traded on the exchanges are actually delivered. This happens because most people make (or lose) money before the contract delivery date actually arrives by buying or selling an offsetting contract to close their position.

FOREIGN CURENCY FUTURES

ADVANTAGES	
Buying Currency	
Profit Potential	The amount of money you can make by buying foreign currency is unlimited.
Small Investment	Since you deposit only a small percentage of the total cost of foreign currency futures, you control large sums of money with a small amount of cash.
Selling Currency	
Profit Potential	The amount that can be made in the foreign currency market is unlimited.
DISADVANTAGES	
Buying Currency	
Unlimited Loss Potential	There is a chance that you could not only lose your total investment, but also be liable for paying out more money.
Time Limitation	You have a limited amount of time to hold a futures contract. If you hold it until it expires, you must take delivery of the currency and pay the balance of the money due.
No Price Limitation	There are no daily limits on price movement. If prices move against you, you might not be able to buy an offsetting contract quickly enough to get out of the market to reduce your losses.
Selling Currency	
Unlimited Loss Potential	The amount of money you can lose is unlimited since you could be required to sell a currency that you do not own for far less than its actual value.
No Price Limitation	There are no daily limits on price movement. If prices move against you, you might not be able to buy an offsetting contract quickly enough to get out of the market to reduce your losses.
Time Limitation	You have a limited amount of time to hold a futures contract. If you hold it until it expires, you must make delivery of the currency.

Limited Partnerships

A **General Partnership** is a business venture where two or more people get together to conduct some type of business. The people in the partnership are considered general partners. That means that they are personally liable for all debts and lawsuits that occur.

A **Limited Partnership** is a business endeavor where there is at least one general partner and one or more limited partners. The difference between the general and limited partners is that, unlike the general partners, limited partners do not run the business and they are not personally liable for debts or lawsuits. The only money that a limited partner can lose is the money they originally invested.

Howard Hughes has a lot of knowledge about real estate and decides to become a developer. He finds a large piece of land that he believes is perfect for building an apartment complex, but needs $1 million to develop the property. Although Howard could create a corporation and sell stock, he chooses not to do so because of the time and expense involved in creating the corporation. Moreover, once the development is complete, there will be no further need for running a corporation. Rather than a corporation, Howard creates a limited partnership with himself as the general partner.

The conditions of the limited partnership state that each share will cost $1,000 and the minimum amount of shares one can purchase is five. After all expenses are paid, the profit will be divided between the general partner and limited partners - 10% for the general partner and 90% for the limited partners. Grace buys ten shares, which means that she invests $10,000.

During the time that the complex is being constructed, Humpty Dumpty, a construction worker, falls off of the building. It is determined that the accident was due to faulty materials that Howard knowingly purchased. Since the accident was Howard's fault, the insurance company decides not to pay for the injury. Humpty Dumpty sues the limited partnership for $500,000 and wins. As a result of the lawsuit, all of the money still held by the limited partnership had to be paid to Humpty. Moreover,

*because the limited partnership only had $200,000 in cash,
Howard is personally liable for paying the remaining $300,000.*

*Howard's incompetence results in Grace and all of the other
limited partners losing their total investment. However, because
they are limited partners, they are not liable for paying the other
$300.000 to Humpty. Additionally, the limited partners can
possibly sue Howard for their money.*

You must be very careful when investing in limited partnerships. Some
of them are good and others are very risky. Unfortunately, there are not
many books that really explain them. This is because each one is
different. The important thing to remember when considering investing
in one is to read all the material provided, ask questions and don't place
your trust in everything that the sales people say - they are trying to sell
you a product. Many sales people will say anything to make the product
look good. They have a talent for reading people and determining what
must be said to get their money. Also, general partners rarely invest their
own money in a venture - they use OPM (other people's money). Plus,
they charge the limited partnership a fee for running the venture, which
means that they receive money even if the limited partnership doesn't
make a dime.

I once found myself in a situation where a company was trying to
convince me to invest in a limited partnership. The tactics used by the
sales people were a lot like those used by car dealerships. There were
three people in a conference room with me, all trying to convince me to
buy. No matter what objections I had, they had a response. I found the
situation to be quite exhilarating because I knew what I would and would
not do. (Of course, I also love negotiating with automobile dealers.)
However, this kind of technique can prove to be very stressful to many
humans. (By the way, I didn't invest.)

LIMITED PARTNERSHIPS

ADVANTAGES	
Unlimited Profit Potential	The profit potential you can realize by investing in Limited Partnerships is unlimited, depending on the partnership.
Limited Loss Potential	You can only lose the money you invest, no more.
DISADVANTAGES	
Access to Your Money	You must wait until the project earns money before you will receive any money. If it does not earn money, you will receive none.
No Control	You have no vote or any other control over how the partnership operates.
Risk	A great deal of risk exists because, while the general partners may have been involved in similar ventures, there is no guarantee that your project will succeed. Also, they are using your money to pay for their management fees.
Liquidity	Limited Partnership shares normally cannot be sold without permission of the general partners. Also, since there is no secondary market, finding a buyer might be very difficult.

Chapter 5
-- Brokers

Brokers are the people who buy and sell stock, options, commodities or other types of financial instruments for individuals and organizations. In exchange for executing the transaction, they receive commissions from their clients. Brokers either work for companies that are members of the exchanges in which they carry out the transactions or they belong to the exchanges themselves. Options brokers belong to option exchanges, Commodity brokers belong to commodities exchanges and Stock brokers belong to stock exchanges. Since brokers are the only ones who can execute transactions on an exchange, you have no choice but to use a broker if you wish to trade. Even if you use your computer to do on-line trading, a broker is still in the picture.

Types of Brokers

The following lists the kinds of brokers that exist, and the functions they serve.

- **Floor Traders** are members of exchanges who trade for their personal accounts rather than for the public. Since they execute their own trades, floor traders pay no transaction costs.

- **Specialists** are exchange members who confine their trading activities to a very small number of securities.

- **Two-Dollar Brokers** are members of a stock exchange who handle transactions for other brokers who are either too busy to trade or absent from the trading floor.

- **Block Traders** are brokers who buy and sell very large amounts of securities, normally for corporations or institutions. They came into being because it was too difficult or expensive for specialists to handle the transactions.

- **Registered Representatives**, also called account executives, are employees of a brokerage firm who takes "buy" and "sell" orders from customers. Once they receive orders, the representatives pass them to the firm's trading floor brokers for execution. When you call to place an order, the person to whom you normally speak is a registered representative.

Services

The brokerage firms with which you have an account will normally fall into one of two categories:

- **Full Service Brokerage** firms are those that, in addition to making trades, will provide research for their customers. They also make suggestions on when to buy or sell, as well as provide clients with news items in the financial world. Furthermore, full service brokers often offer products not available through discount brokers.

- **Discount Brokerage** firms are those that provide only the service of executing trades. People normally use them when they follow the markets closely and are not in need of the other services provided by full service brokers. Normally, these brokers neither make suggestions to their customers nor do they provide research.

Discount brokers have been given that name because their fees are supposed to be lower than full service brokers. I use the word "supposed" because in some instances a discount broker's fee is much greater than that charged by a full service broker. If you wish to buy or sell a large amount of penny stocks, a discount broker may not be the best choice to make because their charges may be based on the number of shares traded. Therefore, if you are selling 5,000 shares at a price of $0.01 per share (a total worth of $50), you could end up pay the broker $100 for selling the stock. I recommend that you not only check the price for trading, but also see if there are additional fees for other services.

A Word of Caution

It is important to realize that brokers are not "all knowing". In fact, the majority brokers you will encounter will be good sales people, but will not know very much about how the financial instruments actually work.

During one point in my career, I decided that I wanted to become a stock broker. I felt that, since I know a lot about the financial markets, I would be a good candidate. I interviewed with a number of the top stock brokerage firms. What I discovered was that the firms did not care about how much I knew about the market. Their only concern was whether or not I could sell. I was hired by Salomon Smith Barney and went through their training program. The training program, which was considered to be one of the best, did not teach trainees anything about analyzing companies or how instruments work. The only thing taught for a period of two weeks was the products that the company offered and how to sell them. We were continually told that when asked a question about the financial markets or investing, we had to have an opinion and give the answer with conviction – it really was not important whether the opinion was correct or whether we actually believed it.

At the end of the training program, in order to be a stockbroker, the trainee has to take a Series 7 examination. If the person passes the examination with a score of at least 70%, they will get their license and can begin trading stock. The exam does not have any questions about how the various financial instruments work. It focused primarily on rules and regulations. In fact, once they pass the exam, most brokers do not remember any of the material they studied to take the test. However, after passing a test, a person is considered a financial expert and wants you to entrust your life savings with them.

Brokers have no crystal ball showing which stocks will soar or decline, or what interest rates will be next year. Most of their advice comes from research performed by the research analysts within the company. Although the information is available to everyone, it takes knowledge to know where to find it and time to interpret it correctly. Don't expect brokers to give you any information that is not available to everyone else.

The Securities and Exchange Commission (SEC) has stringent laws governing the dissemination of "inside" information. Moreover, if information is leaked to a broker ahead of time, the first people to receive it, and therefore who have a chance to act on the information, will be the broker's larger clients. I feel confident in saying that by the time you receive information, quite a few others already have the same knowledge and have had an opportunity to act upon it.

Brokers make their money from the transaction fees received from buy and selling securities for their clients and from interest charged on margin accounts. As a result, they tend to cater more to people who do a lot of trading or have large sums of money to invest. Be cautious in your dealings with them. I am not saying that all brokers are out to steal you blind or that they know nothing about their craft. They can, and do, make suggestions, but take no responsibility for any losses that you incur. Except under predefined circumstances, you are under no obligation to follow a broker's suggestion. I have encountered brokers that, while doing nothing unethical, definitely did not have their client's interest in mind. All of the brokers that I know work solely on commissions. As a result, if you don't buy or sell, they make no money.

In defense of brokers' actions and attitudes, you should consider your own motives for calling them in the first place. You are using this human as a tool. In most cases, if people could trade without using a broker, they probably would. You contact the broker only when you feel it is beneficial to you. You buy stocks, trade options or sell futures only because you feel that doing so will make you money, not because there is a broker out there who has a family to feed. In turn, the broker is serving you because he wants to make money, not because it gives him a warm, fuzzy feeling inside. Unfortunately, the Lone Ranger and Robin Hood have retired.

An Even Bigger Word of Caution

In Chapter 3, I warned that sometimes the top management of large companies lie about the performance of their company to make the company look better to investors, which result in bigger bonuses to the managers.. This situation is also true about the major financial services companies, which include banks.

Many of the brokers who provide information to their customers get their information and recommendations from their research departments. During my training class at Salomon Smith Barney, we were taught how to sell and told to rely on the company's reseach departments to provide technical information and recommendations. The financial crisis that occurred in 1980's, the one in the early 2000's and the latest one in 2008 all lead back to financial services companies engaging in fraudulent activities and using investors' money to finance their risky deals. In most cases, the U.S. government bailed out the financial institutions, but the investors still lost.

In 2003, the U.S. Securities and Exchange Commission (SEC) filed a claim against Salomon Smith Barney. The lawsuit included issuing "…research reports on two telecommunications ("telecom") companies that were fraudulent and issued research reports on several telecom companies that violated NASD and NYSE rules regulating their members' communications with the public…" This was not the only lawsuit and not the only major financial services firm that engaged in those practices.

Keep in mind that the brokers you deal with directly are not the people responsible for many of these fradulent and unethical activities – these practices are done and approved by top management. Your broker might be genuinely concerned about helping you to make money. When making suggestions about investing in various instruments, they are relying on the information they receive from the analysts and experts in their company.

Unfortunately, when things like the financial meltdown, the bankruptcy of Lehman Brothers and other scandals occur, the investors are the ones losing the money and the retail brokers are the people who get all of the telephone calls from their clients. The brokers are expected to answer the hard questions when, in fact, the brokers were just following the direction and using the expertise provided by their company.

Chapter 6
-- Conclusion

The method you use to increase your income depends on your goals. You must decide whether to invest or speculate. If you wish to build a "nest egg" for retirement, you have the option of investing in money market funds; mutual funds; bonds; blue chip stocks; certificates of deposits; or treasury bills, notes, or bonds. All of these investments yield moderate rates of return and are relatively safe. If you wish to try getting bigger gains, a number of speculative alternatives are available. Instruments such as commodities, speculative stocks, foreign currencies and options can be used. As previously mentioned, although large sums of money can be made, they can also be lost. If your primary goal is to have quick access to your money while still getting the highest possible yield, money market funds may be the most viable choice.

If you are interested in investing in any of the instruments discussed in this book, especially options, commodities or foreign currency, I strongly advise that you get books on the subject. The more you know about how an investment works and the kinds of strategies that can be used, the greater your chances of success. Also, it will give you a better idea of whether you really should venture down that particular investment road.

The investment vehicles discussed in this book are by no means all of the ones available. New ways of investing are always being introduced, while other methods are being discontinued. In the introduction, I described the difference between safe investing and speculative investing by relaying the story of the $100 received by Jim Hankins and Ron Turner. In the story, Jim took a big chance for big gains and big losses. Ron, on the other hand, chose smaller gains and a small chance of losing. What I did not previously mention is what Michelle Ventour decided to do with her $100.

Just like Jim and Ron. Michelle received $100 from her father. She did not want to put all of her money into an account paying only 5% interest like Ron because she would not see any gains for a long time. Moreover, Michelle did not want to put all of her money into a lemonade business like Jim did because she might lose it all. What she decided to do was to put $50 into a saving account and investing the other $50 in Jim's lemonade stand. By doing so, Jim has more money to buy the items needed for the stand and Michelle had an opportunity to make money if the stand does well.

In the previous example, Michelle decided to "diversify." That is, she has chosen to invest her money in more than one area. She is assured of a small gain from the money in the savings account and has a chance to make a larger gain if the lemonade stand is a success. If the stand in not successful, Michelle will not lose everything.

I suggest that you don't invest like Jim - putting all of your money in high risk instruments, nor like Ron - putting all of it in instruments that tie your investment up for a long time. I strongly feel that Michelle's method of investing is the best way. Although you will not make money as quickly by using this approach, you will be able to sleep a little easier at night.

The Importance of Early Investing

Rather than investing while they are young, many people decide to have fun early and start saving and investing money at a much later date. After all, there is plenty of time to think about saving. However, what most people don't consider is that if they start early with a small amount of money, it is possible to make as much or more than if they invest a lot more later. Consider the following example.

Cain and Abel Jones are twins. They laugh alike. They walk alike. At times, they even talk alike. You could lose your mind. After they began working at the same company, Cain decides to deposit money into an Individual Retirement Account (IRA). Abel chooses to wait and have fun with his money. After eight years of watching Cain save money in his IRA, Abel decides to open an IRA and start saving. In contrast, Cain decides that is was time to start having more fun and stop putting money in his IRA. The following shows what happened to the two brothers' money, assuming that they receive a return of 10% per year.

CONCLUSION

Age	Cain's investment		Abel's Investment	
	Deposit Made	Amount Accumulated	Deposit Made	Amount Accumulated
19	$2.000	$2.000	$0	$0
20	$2,000	$4,200	$0	$0
21	$2,000	$6,620	$0	$0
22	$2,000	$9,282	$0	$0
23	$2,000	$12,210	$0	$0
24	$2,000	$15,431	$0	$0
25	$2,000	$18,974	$0	$0
26	$2,000	$22,872	$0	$0
27	$0	$25,159	$2,000	$2,000
28	$0	$27,675	$2,000	$4,200
29	$0	$30,442	$2,000	$6,620
30	$0	$33,487	$2,000	$9,282
31	$0	$36,835	$2,000	$12,210
32	$0	$40,519	$2,000	$15,431
33	$0	$44,571	$2,000	$18,974
34	$0	$49,028	$2,000	$22,872
35	$0	$53,930	$2,000	$27,159
36	$0	$59,323	$2,000	$31,875
37	$0	$65,256	$2,000	$37,062
38	$0	$71,781	$2,000	$42,769
39	$0	$78,960	$2,000	$49,045
40	$0	$86,856	$2,000	$55,950
41	$0	$95,541	$2,000	$63,545
42	$0	$105,095	$2,000	$71,899
43	$0	$115,605	$2,000	$81,089
44	$0	$127,165	$2,000	$91,198
45	$0	$139,882	$2,000	$102,318
46	$0	$153,870	$2,000	$114,550
47	$0	$169,257	$2,000	$128,005
48	$0	$186,183	$2,000	$142,805
49	$0	$204,801	$2,000	$159,086
50	$0	$225,281	$2,000	$176,995
51	$0	$247,809	$2,000	$196,694
52	$0	$272,590	$2,000	$218,364
53	$0	$299,849	$2,000	$242,200
54	$0	$329,834	$2,000	$268,420
55	$0	$362,817	$2,000	$297,262
56	$0	$399,099	$2,000	$328,988
57	$0	$439,009	$2,000	$363,887
58	$0	$482,910	$2,000	$402,276
59	$0	$531,201	$2,000	$444,503

Total investment   Cain $14,000   Abel $80,000

Total Return   Cain $531,201   Abel $444,503

In the previous example, Abel invested a total of $80,000 and accumulated $444,000, which is not too bad. However, by starting out seven years earlier, Cain invested only $14,000 and accumulated $531,000. Obviously, if Cain continued to put money into his IRA for more than eight years, he would have more than twice as much as his brother.

Keeping Score

When his team was down three games to one in the championship playoffs, NBA coach Dick Motta once stated, "The opera ain't over 'til the fat lady sings." That also holds true for investing. When you own stock or have money invested in other areas, although the price may rise or fall, you are only making or losing money on paper. That is, if you buy a share of stock for $1 and it rises to $50, you are not $49 richer unless you actually sell the stock. Likewise, if the stock falls to 20¢, you have not actually lost 80¢ until you sell it. That is why the Internal Revenue Service doesn't have its hand held out to collect taxes until you sell the stock.

The reason that people invest is to make as much money as possible. However, a problem arises when a person realizes that, after letting $250 sit in an account for three months, they have only earned $7.25. What is not realized is that the $7.25 represents 11½ percent interest, which is more than three times greater than the interest paid by banks.

The point that I am trying to make is that the object of the game is to make the most money from what you've got. I remember a poem I recited when I played the roll of "Penny Bright" in a kid's play. Some might think it to be a bit corny (because it is), but I like it anyway.

> *Rack 'em up and stack 'em up*
> *And stash your cash away.*
> *Sunshine's daylight savings time*
> *Before that rainy day.*
>
> *In the bank the dollars grow.*
> *The bank book tells how many.*
> *But every dollar, crisp and green*
> *Started with a penny.*

Appendix A
-- Invest or Not Invest

Invest, or not invest. That is the question.

Whether 'tis wiser in the mind to place your money into financial instruments

Or suffer the slings and arrows of no interest

By leaving it stuffed in your mattress.

The heartache and the thousand natural shocks when seeing a high risk investment losing money;

To invest in low risk instruments, perchance to dream;

For in that investment you can get peaceful sleep by not worrying about the risk.

R. N. Smith

The following pages contain flow charts designed to show what investment options are available based on your goals. By answering each question and following the appropriate legs of the charts, you will be lead to the investments that address your needs. If you believe in diversifying, you will probably find it necessary to follow more than one leg of the chart. This has not been presented to suggest one instrument over another, just to give an overall picture of all the investments discussed in this book.

Investment Decision Chart

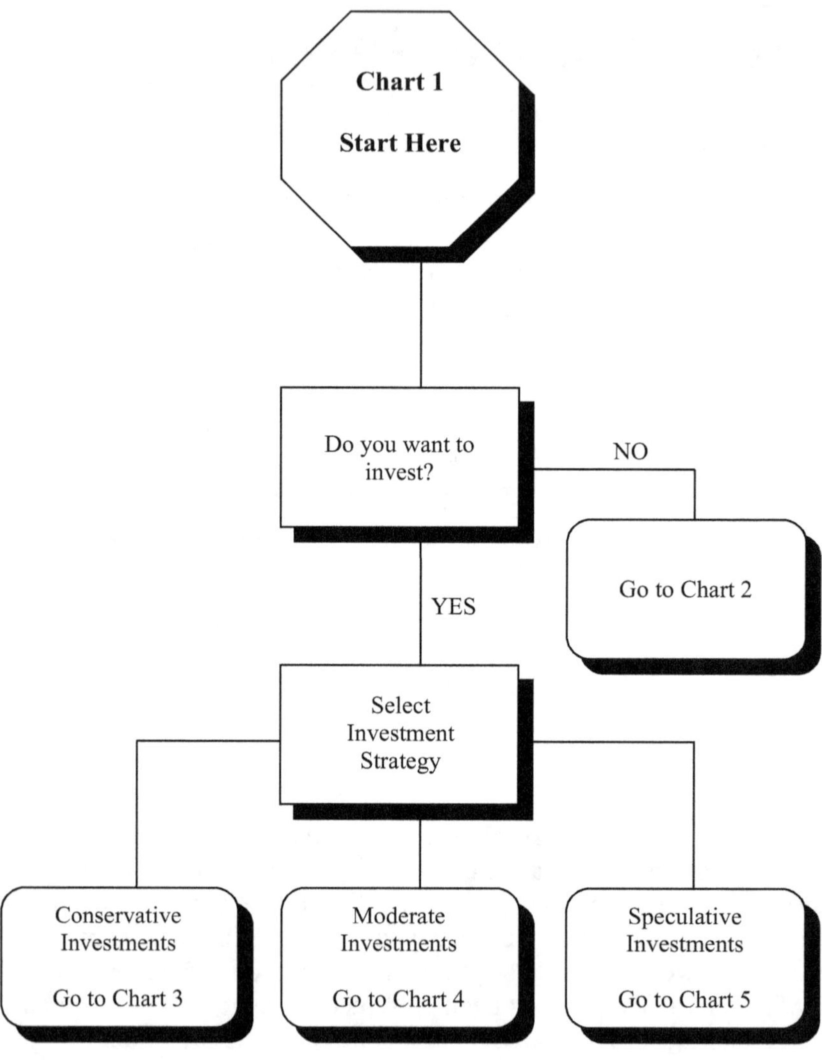

Investment Decision Chart

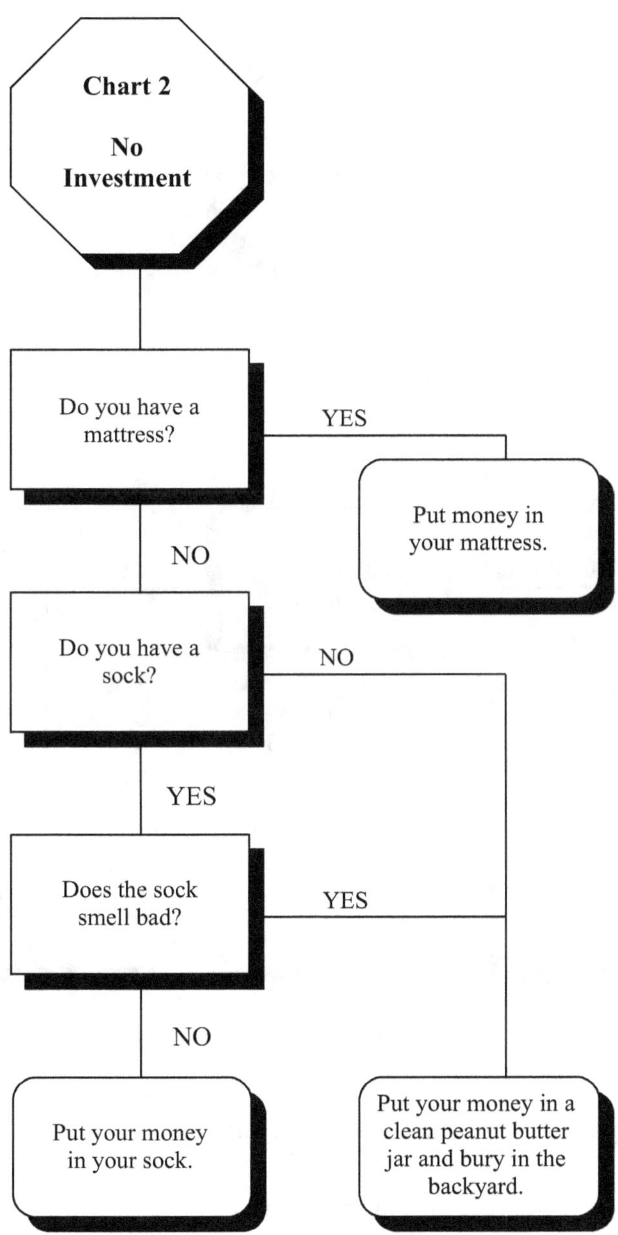

Investment Decision Chart

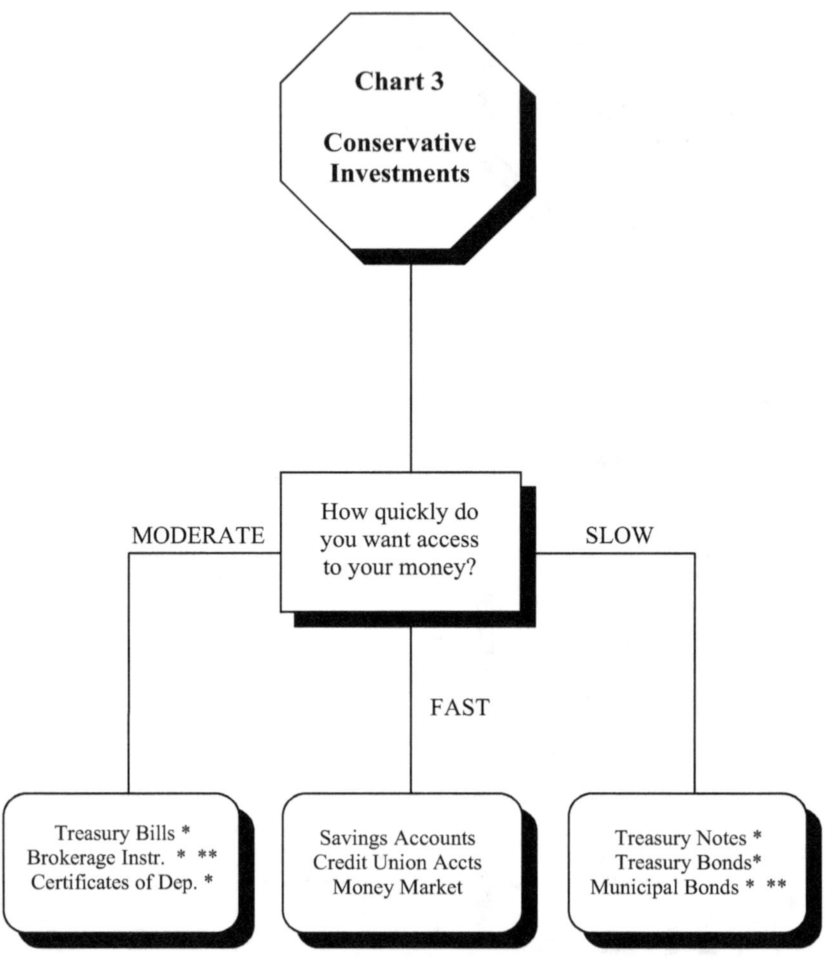

*　　These Instruments can possibly be turned into cash quickly if sold prior to maturity in the secondary market using a brokerage firm.

**　Conservative depending on bond rating.

Investment Decision Chart

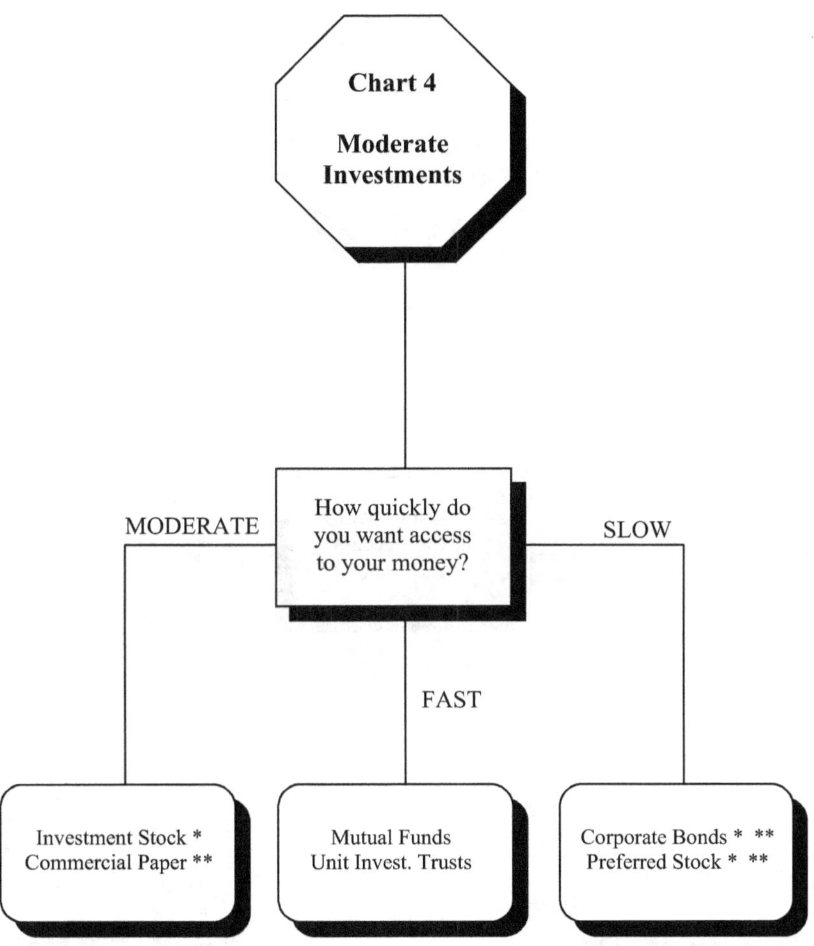

*   These instruments can possibly be turned into cash relatively fast if sold prior to maturity by using a brokerage firm.

**   Moderate Investment depending on credit rating.

Investment Decision Chart

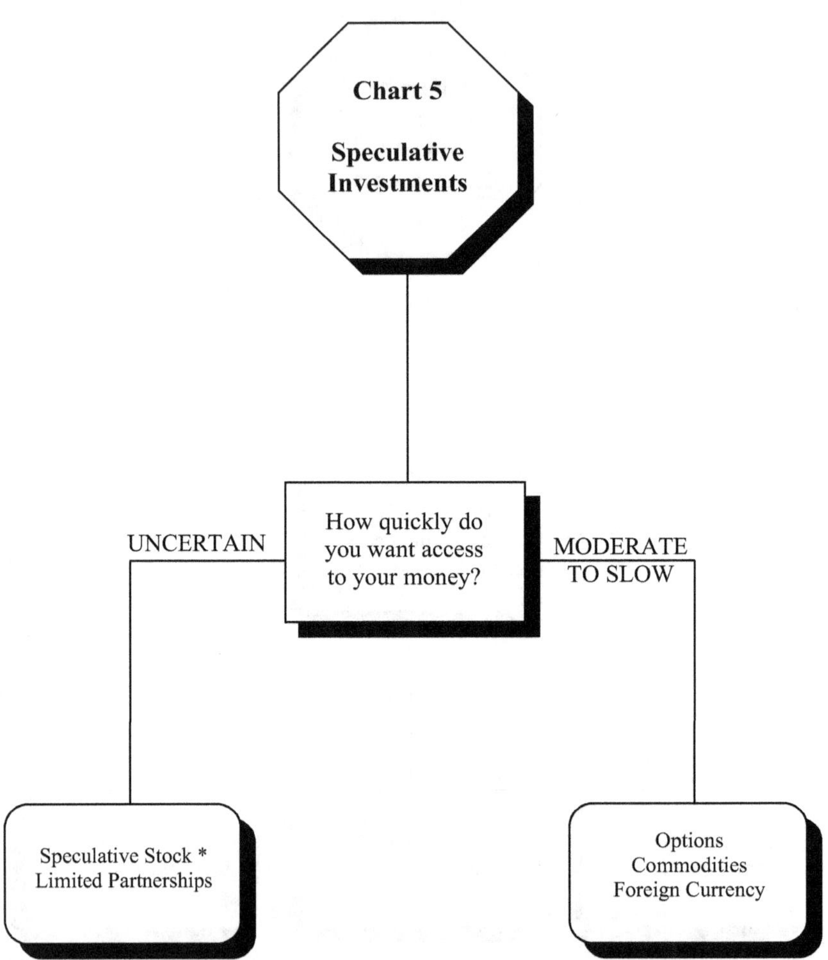

* Liquidity depends on stock.

Appendix B
-- Bond Pricing Explored

Bonds are different from many other financial instruments because you buy them at a price that is greater than, less than or equal to the face value. Then, at predetermined times, you receive the face value plus any other amounts previously agreed upon. Therefore, to determine the value of bonds, you must calculate their present value at the time they are purchased. The present value of a bond represents how much the investment is worth today when you take in consideration the face value that is paid at maturity and the interest payments made throughout the life of the bond. The present value of a $1,000 bond that matures in 15 years and pays 15% interest is not the same as one paying 15% interest, but that matures in 5 years. You pay less for the 15 year bond than for the 5 year one. It is fairly easy to figure out exactly how much less. The following example will show you how it is done. There are also charts in Appendices C and D to aid in the calculations.

On January 1, 1975 Harry S. Truman buys a $1,000 bond paying 16% interest. It will mature on December 31, 1990. He must calculate how much must be paid for the bond. To do so, Harry first calculates the present value of the bond's $1,000 face value. Since his bond, like most, pays interest twice a year and there will be 15 years of interest payments, if he keeps it for the full time there will be a total of 30 payments. Also, he knows that, because there are two payments a year, the interest being paid is actually 8% every six months. Since Harry doesn't have a copy of the charts in Appendix C, he uses the formula:

Present Value of face = $f \times 1 / (1 + r)^n$

f = face value of bond ($1,000)

r = interest rate of a single payment (16% / 2 = 8% or .08)

n = number of total payments if held until maturity

(15 years x 2 payments per year = 30 payments)

Plugging in the values we get:

$$\text{Present Value of face} = \$1{,}000 \times 1 / (1 + .08)^{30}$$
$$= \$1{,}000 \times 1 / (1.08)^{30}$$
$$= \$1{,}000 \times 1 / 10.062613$$
$$= \$1{,}000 \times .099377$$
$$= \$99.38$$

If Harry buys the $1,000, 16% bond and received no interest payments for the next 15 years, it would cost $99.38. On December 31, 1990 he would get $1,000 from the company that issued the bond. Since interest payments are made every six months, the present value of those payments must also be added to the purchase price. However, before he can calculate the present value of the interest payments, Harry must know how much he will receive every six months. To do so, he uses the equation:

$$\text{Payment} = f \times r$$

f = face value of bond ($1,000)

r = interest rate of a single payment (16% / 2 = 8% or .08)

$$\text{Payment} = \$1{,}000 \times .08$$
$$= \$80$$

Harry will receive $80 every six months for the next 15 years. The $80 interest payments also have a present value. Therefore, because he doesn't have a copy of Appendix D to figure out the present value of the interest payments, Harry uses the equation:

$$\text{Present value of coupon} = c \times (1 - (1 / (1 + r)^{n})) / r$$

c = amount of one coupon payment ($80)

r = interest rate of a Single payment (16% / 2 = 8% or .08)

n = number of total payments if held until maturity
(15 years x 2 payments per year = 30 payments)

Plugging in the values we get:

PV of coupon   = $80 x (1 - (1 / (1 + .08)^{30})) / .08
               = $80 x (1 - (1 / (1.08)^{30})) / .08
               = $80 x (1 - (1 / 10.062613)) / .08
               = $80 x (1 - 0.099378) / .08
               = $80 x .900623 / .08
               = $80 x 11.25778
               = $900.62

If Harry buys a $1,000, 16% bond, receives interest payments for 15 years, but <u>does not</u> get the $1,000 lump sum at the end of the period, he will have to pay $900.62. Since both the lump sum and the interest are paid, the present value of the two must be added together to determine how much to pay for the bonds.

Present value of face value	$ 99.38
Present value of coupon payments	+ $ 900.62
Total to pay for bond	$1,000.00

Harry must pay $1,000 for the bond. If he holds it for the total amount of time, he will receive the $1,000 face value plus 30 interest payments of $80 each, for a total of $2,400.

As previously stated, a bond paying the same interest rate, with a shorter maturity date has a different present value. This results in the holder possibly paying the same face value, receiving the face value when it matures, but making less interest.

Fred G. Sanford buys a $1,000 bond paying 16% interest on January 1, 1985. Like Harry's bond, Fred's bond will expire on December 31, 1990. Moreover, he will pay the same amount that Harry paid for the bond.

Now, you are probably saying to yourself "...holy smoke!!! Why are Fred and Harry paying the same amount for a bond when Harry held his 10 years longer than Fred??? It isn't fair! It isn't fair!" Don't allow this debilitating debacle to devour your docile demeanor. There is still justice in the world. Although Fred will receive an $80 interest payment every six months like Harry, the total number of payments will be less. Remember, Harry is *holding his bond for 15 years, which results in him receiving 30 coupon payments totaling $2,400. In contrast, Fred will only be holding his bond for five years, which results in him receiving only ten coupon payments totaling $800.*

Present Value of face $= f \times 1 / (1 + r)^n$

f = face value of bond ($1,000)

r = interest rate of a single payment (16% / 2 = 8% or .08)

n = number of total payments if held until maturity
(5 years x 2 payments per year = 10 payments)

Plugging in the values we get:

$$
\begin{aligned}
\text{Present Value of face} \quad &= \$1,000 \times 1 / (1 + .08)^{10} \\
&= \$1,000 \times 1 / (1.08)^{10} \\
&= \$1,000 \times 1 / 2.158925 \\
&= \$1,000 \times .4631935 \\
&= \$463.19
\end{aligned}
$$

The present value of Fred's bond is $463.19, which means that he will pay that amount for it if there are no coupon payments. Since he will receive the $80 semi-annual coupon payments, the present value of the interest payments must also be calculated.

Present value of coupon $= c \times (1 - (1 / (1 + r)^n)) / r$

c = amount of one coupon payment ($80)

r = interest rate of a single payment (16% / 2 = 8% or .08)

n = number of total payments if held until maturity
(5 years x 2 payments per year = 10 payments)

Plugging in the values we get:

$$
\begin{aligned}
\text{PV of coupon} \quad &= \$80 \times (1 - (1 / (1 + .08)^{10})) / .08 \\
&= \$80 \times (1 - (1 / (1.08)^{10})) / .08 \\
&= \$80 \times (1 - (1 / 2.158925)) / .08
\end{aligned}
$$

$$= \$80 \times (1 - .4631935) / .08$$
$$= \$80 \times .5368065 / .08$$
$$= \$80 \times 6.7100813$$
$$= \$536.81$$

Adding the present value of the face value to the present value of the coupons will show that Fred will also pay the same price for the bond as Harry paid.

Present value of face value	$ 463.19
Present value of coupon payments	+ $ 536.81
	————
Total to pay for bond	$1,000.00

The total amount Fred will receive from the interest payments is $800 ($80 x 10 payments), which is quite less than the $2,400 that Harry will receive.

As you may have guessed by now, the amount that you pay for a bond is equivalent to the face value of the bond. The length of time in which you hold the bond will determine the amount of interest that will be received.

If a company issuing bonds has the same credit rating throughout the life of the bond, has the same net worth and the economy is the same, the price of the bond will probably always sell for the amount of the face value. However, there is a greater chance that someone will discover Elvis running a Motel 6 in Tupello, Mississippi than a company and the economy staying the same for 15 years. Therefore, quite often, the interest rate stated on the face of a bond is not the same as the one people are willing to pay.

Bull Winkle decides to buy a newly issued $1,000 AT&T bond that pays 16% interest and matures five years from the date of purchase. He knows that, because AT&T has a credit rating that will allow it to borrow at a rate of 10% interest, he will have to pay more than the face value. Since he wants to know how much the bond will actually cost, Bull decides to calculate the price.

He first calculates the present value of the face amount:

Present Value of face $= f \times 1 / (1 + r)^n$

f $\quad=$ face value of bond ($1,000)

r $\quad=$ interest rate of a single payment (10% / 2 = 5% or .05)

n $\quad=$ number of total payments if held until maturity

(5 years x 2 payments per year = 10 payments)

Plugging in the values we get:

$$
\begin{aligned}
\text{Present Value of interest} \quad &= \$1{,}000 \times 1 / (1 + .05)^{10} \\
&= \$1{,}000 \times 1 / (1.05)^{10} \\
&= \$1{,}000 \times 1 / 1.6288946 \\
&= \$1{,}000 \times .6139133 \\
&= \$613.91
\end{aligned}
$$

The present value of the bond's face value calculated at 10% is $613.91. (The 10% interest rate is used instead of the original 16% because 10% is the actual amount of interest being paid by the firm.)

The amount of the interest payments is still based on the original interest rate and face value.

Payment $= f \times r$

f $=$ face value of bond ($1,000)

r $=$ interest rate of a single payment (16% / 2 = 8% or .08)

$$
\begin{aligned}
\text{Payment} \quad &= \$1000 \times .08 \\
&= \$80
\end{aligned}
$$

The present value of Bull's interest payments, like the present value of the bond's face, is based on the interest rate the company will actually be paying, which is 10% rather than 16%:

Present value of coupon $= c \times (1 - (1 / (1 + r)^n)) / r$

c = amount of one coupon payment ($80)

r = Interest rate of a single payment (10% / 2 = 5% or .05)

n = number of total payments if held until maturity
(5 years x 2 payments per year = 10 payments)

$$
\begin{aligned}
\text{PV of coupon} \quad &= \$80 \times (1 - (1 / (1 + .05)^{10})) / .05 \\
&= \$80 \times (1 - (1 / (1.05)^{10})) / .05 \\
&= \$80 \times (1 - (1 / 1.628891)) / .05 \\
&= \$80 \times (1 - 0.613914) / .05 \\
&= \$80 \times 0.386086 / .05 \\
&= \$80 \times 7.721720 \\
&= \$617.74
\end{aligned}
$$

Adding the present value of the interest that the company is actually paying to the value of the coupons shows that Bull will have to pay more than the face value indicates.

Present value of face value (adjusted)	$ 613.91
Present value of coupon payments	+ $ 617.74
Total to pay for bond	$1,231.65

The total amount Bull will receive from the interest payments is:

$80 x 10 payments = $800

Since the coupon payments are based on 16% interest and the company is actually paying 10%, if Bull pays the face value, he will actually receive $231.65 more than he is due. AT&T avoids paying Bull more than he is actually due is by collecting more than the face value of the bond, which is $231.65 more, to be exact.

The previous example illustrates why you might have to pay more for a bond than the face value. In the next example we will look at why you might pay less than the face value.

Jim Beam wants to buy a GTE $1,000, 16% bond with a maturity 5 years from that date. However, Jim doesn't know how much it will cost because the firm's credit rating only allows them to borrow at 20% interest. He decides to calculate the cost of the bond.

He first calculates the present value of the face amount:

Present Value of face = f x 1 / (1 + r) ^{n}

f = face value of bond ($1,000)

r = interest rate of a Single payment (20% / 2 = 5% or .10)

n = number of total payments if held until maturity
    (5 years x 2 payments per year = 10 payments)

Plugging in the values we get:

$$\begin{aligned}
\text{Present Value of interest} &= \$1,000 \times 1 / (1 + .10)^{10} \\
&= \$1,000 \times 1 / (1.10)^{10} \\
&= \$1,000 \times 1 / 2.5937423 \\
&= \$1,000 \times .3855433 \\
&= \$385.54
\end{aligned}$$

The present value of the bond's face value, calculated at 20%, is $385.54. The 20% interest rate is used instead of the original 16% because 20% is the actual amount of interest being paid by the firm.

The amount of the interest payments is still based on the original interest rate and face value.

Payment = f x r

f = face value of bond ($1,000)

r = interest rate of a single payment (16% / 2 = 8% or .08)

$$\begin{aligned}
\text{Payment} &= \$1,000 \times .08 \\
&= \$80
\end{aligned}$$

The present value of Jim's interest payments, like the present value of the bond's face, will be based on the interest rate the company will actually be paying, which is 20% rather than 16%:

Present value of coupon = c x (1 - (1 / (1 + r) ^{n})) / r

c = amount of one coupon payment ($80)

r = interest rate of a single payment (20% / 2 = 10% or .10)

n = number of total payments if held until maturity
   (5 years x 2 payments per year = 10 payments)

Plugging in the values we get:

$$
\begin{aligned}
\text{PV of coupon} \quad &= \$80 \times (1 - (1 / (1 + .10)^{10})) / .10 \\
&= \$80 \times (1 - (1 / (1.10)^{10})) / .10 \\
&= \$80 \times (1 - (1 / 2.5937423)) / .10 \\
&= \$80 \times (1 - 0.3855433) / .10 \\
&= \$80 \times 0.6144567 / .10 \\
&= \$80 \times 6.144567 \\
&= \$491.57
\end{aligned}
$$

Adding the present value of the interest the company is actually paying to the present value of the coupons shows that Jim will pay less than the face value indicates.

Present value of face value (adjusted)	$ 385.54
Present value of coupon payments	+ $ 491.56
Total to pay for bond	$ 877.10

The total amount Jim will receive from the interest payments is:

$80 x 10 payments = $800

Since the coupon payments are based on 16% interest and GTE is actually paying 20%, if Jim pays the face amount of the bond, he will actually receive $122.90 less than he is due. GTE avoids having to give Jim a refund when the bond matures by charging him $122.90 less than the face value.

Appendix C
-- Present Value Tables

The following tables show the present value of $1.00. The formula used to calculate a present value is:

$$\text{Present Value} = f \times 1 / (1 + r)^n$$

f = amount of payment at maturity ($1.00)

r = interest rate of a single payment

n = number of total payments

Using the tables is a quick and easy way of calculating the present values without using the formula. If you want to impress your friends and family or show your significant other that you are not just another pretty face, but have a brain too, whip out your calculator and use the formula. Otherwise, use the tables.

Richard and Pat Nixon just became the proud parents of a baby boy. They named him Checkers because Richard happened to be playing chess when the baby was born. (Richard decided against the name Chess because he felt that it would be a ridiculous name for a baby.)

One afternoon after Pat came home from the hospital with Checkers, she and Richard began discussing Checkers' future. "Well Dickey," stated Pat, "what do you think Checkers will be when he grows up?"

"I don't know, but if he is going to be President, Checkers needs to go to a good university, like the University of Chicago or Harvard. By the time he turns eighteen, tuition at either of those places will be at least $200,000. Therefore, we have to be sure that he will have money to go to school."

"I know," said Pat. "Why don't we buy a zero coupon bond that will pay us $200,000 in eighteen years? That way, Checkers future will be guaranteed."

"Good idea, Honey Bunny," replied Richard. "In fact, I know where we can buy a bond that will pay 9% interest per year. I will calculate how much we'll have to spend for a bond that will pay us $200,000 in 18 years."

Richard began to calculate how much money he will have to invest. To determine the amount that must be invested, Richard goes down the present value chart to the line showing 18 periods, which is the number of years in which interest will be paid. He then goes across to the column that shows 9%, which is the amount of interest that will be paid during the 18-year period. The number shown is .2120, which is the present value of a dollar. Richard then multiplies the number by $200,000, which is the amount that he wants to be paid at the end of the 18-year period. The result is $42,400, which is what he must invest.

Had Richard been able to receive 12% interest on the investment, he would have to invest $26,000. If he received only 5% interest, Richard would have invested $83,100.

Present Value Tables (1% to 6%)						
No. of Periods	**1%**	**2%**	**3%**	**4%**	**5%**	**6%**
1	.9901	.9804	.9709	.9615	.9524	.9434
2	.9803	.9612	.9426	.9246	.9070	.8900
3	.9706	.9423	.9151	.8890	.8638	.8396
4	.9610	.9238	.8885	.8548	.8227	.7921
5	.9515	.9057	.8626	.8219	.7835	.7473
6	.9420	.8880	.8375	.7903	.7462	.7050
7	.9327	.8706	.8131	.7599	.7107	.6651
8	.9235	.8535	.7894	.7307	.6768	.6274
9	.9143	.8368	.7664	.7026	.6446	.5919
10	.9053	.8203	.7441	.6756	.6139	.5584
11	.8963	.8043	.7224	.6496	.5847	.5268
12	.8874	.7885	.7014	.6246	.5568	.4970
13	.8787	.7730	.6810	.6006	.5303	.4688
14	.8700	.7579	.6611	.5775	.5051	.4423
15	.8613	.7430	.6419	.5553	.4810	.4173
16	.8528	.7284	.6232	.5339	.4581	.3936
17	.8444	.7142	.6050	.5134	.4363	.3714
18	.8360	.7002	.5874	.4936	.4155	.3503
19	.8277	.6864	.5703	.4746	.3957	.3305
20	.8195	.6730	.5537	.4564	.3769	.3118
25	.7798	.6095	.4776	.3751	.2953	.2330
30	.7419	.5521	.4120	.3083	.2314	.1741

Present Value Tables (7% to 14%)

No. of Periods	7%	8%	9%	10%	12%	14%
1	.9346	.9259	.9174	.9091	.8929	.8772
2	.8734	.8573	.8417	.8264	.7972	.7695
3	.8163	.7938	.7722	.7513	.7118	.6750
4	.7629	.7350	.7084	.6830	.6355	.5921
5	.7130	.6806	.6499	.6209	.5674	.5194
6	.6663	.6302	.5963	.5645	.5066	.4556
7	.6227	.5835	.5470	.5132	.4523	.3996
8	.5820	.5403	.5019	.4665	.4039	.3506
9	.5439	.5002	.4604	.4241	.3606	.3075
10	.5083	.4632	.4224	.3855	.3220	.2697
11	.4751	.4289	.3875	.3505	.2875	.2366
12	.4440	.3971	.3555	.3186	.2567	.2076
13	.4150	.3677	.3262	.2897	.2292	.1821
14	.3878	.3405	.2992	.2633	.2046	.1597
15	.3624	.3152	.2745	.2394	.1827	.1401
16	.3387	.2919	.2519	.2176	.1631	.1229
17	.3166	.2703	.2311	.1978	.1456	.1078
18	.2959	.2502	.2120	.1799	.1300	.0946
19	.2765	.2317	.1945	.1635	.1161	.0829
20	.2584	.2145	.1784	.1486	.1037	.0728
25	.1842	.1460	.1160	.0923	.0588	.0378
30	.1314	.0994	.0754	.0573	.0334	.0196

Present Value Tables (15% to 36%)

No. of Periods	15%	16%	18%	20%	24%	36%
1	.9901	.9804	.9709	.9615	.9524	.9434
2	.9803	.9612	.9426	.9246	.9070	.8900
3	.9706	.9423	.9151	.8890	.8638	.8396
4	.9610	.9238	.8885	.8548	.8227	.7921
5	.4972	.4761	.4371	.4019	.3411	.2149
6	.4323	.4104	.3704	.3349	.2751	.1580
7	.3759	.3538	.3139	.2791	.2218	.1162
8	.3269	.3050	.2660	.2326	.1789	.0854
9	.2843	.2630	.2255	.1938	.1443	.0628
10	.2472	.2267	.1911	.1615	.1164	.0462
11	.2149	.1954	.1619	.1346	.0938	.0340
12	.1869	.1685	.1372	.1122	.0757	.0250
13	.1625	.1452	.1163	.0935	.0610	.0184
14	.1413	.1252	.0985	.0779	.0492	.0135
15	.1229	.1079	.0835	.0649	.0397	.0099
16	.1069	.0930	.0708	.0541	.0320	.0073
17	.0929	.0802	.0600	.0451	.0258	.0054
18	.0808	.0691	.0508	.0376	.0208	.0039
19	.0703	.0596	.0431	.0313	.0168	.0029
20	.0611	.0514	.0365	.0261	.0135	.0021
25	.0304	.0245	.0160	.0105	.0046	.0005
30	.0151	.0116	.0070	.0042	.0016	.0001

Appendix D
-- Present Value of an Annuity

The following tables show the present value of an annuity of $1.00. An **annuity** is a series of payments of a fixed amount for a specified number of periods. Each payment is received at the end of the period. Coupon payments that you receive when buying bonds are considered an annuity. The formula used to calculate the present value of an annuity is:

$$\text{PV of an Annuity} = c \times (1 - (1 / (1 + r)^n)) / r$$

c = amount of one payment ($1.00)

r = interest rate of a single payment

n = number of total payments

Using the tables is an easy way of calculating the present values without using the formula.

Betsy Ross, the Mayor of Royal Comfort, Nevada was sitting at her kitchen table with her cat Spot trying to figure out how the town could raise money. Her husband, the previous Mayor, ran away with a traveling saleswoman and with all the money in the city treasury. After hours of thinking, drinking ten cups of coffee and eating three slices of two-day old pizza, she decides that the city can hold a lottery in which people will have to select five numbers out of thirty to win a jackpot. Everyone who has the winning combination will share in a jackpot of $1 million. The price of entering the lottery will be $1.00 per ticket.

Initially, Betsy was a happy as a pig in a tub of chicken fat because she was sure that based on lotteries in other states, many people will want to enter. However, her happiness soon turned to grief as she realized that, for the city to make any money, well over a million people will have to buy tickets. Betsy feels that the city can sell a million tickets, but isn't certain that it can sell many more than that amount. Suddenly, she gets an idea – an ANNUITY!!!

Rather than paying the lottery winners $1 million immediately, she will pay them $100,000 a year for ten years. After finishing her fourth slice of pizza, Betsy calls a meeting of the city council to present her idea. When her presentation is complete, Councilman Paul Revere asks Betsy "...what difference does it make whether we pay them $1 million now or over a ten year period? If we only sell a million tickets, we will still only have $1 million. Since the city will be getting nothing out of the deal, why should we waste our time making some other jerk rich? That's a ridiculous idea."

"You twit," replied Betsy. "What do you think I'm proposing to do? I'm not suggesting that we let the money sit in a shoe box over the ten years and take it out when we have to pay the winners. We can pay them $100,000 the first year, and then buy an annuity to cover the rest of the payments."

"What is an annuity?" asked Paul.

"You twit," replied Betsy. "An annuity is a stream of payments that are made in arrears."

"In my ears?" asked Paul.

"You twit," replied Betsy. "I said 'in arrears', not 'in your ears'. Look, all we have to do is buy an insurance policy, a bond or some other financial instrument that pays interest. The most important thing is that it pays us $100,000 per year for nine years. That way, we will be able to pay the lottery winners."

"Okay, we will not have to give the lottery winner $1,000,000. Instead, we will give the lottery winners $100,000 and then give an insurance company $900,000. What's the point? We still will not have any money."

"You twit!" replied Betsy. "The insurance company, the bond or whatever instrument we use will be paying us interest for investing with them. Each year they will give us $100,000, and we will pay the winners. Since we will be receiving interest over the nine-year period, we will not have to spend $900,000 for the annuity. We will only have to pay an amount sufficient enough to

cover the annuity. Therefore, the money that the city has remaining from the purchase can go into the treasury."

"Groovy!" replied Paul. "How much do we have to spend for the annuity?"

"You twit!" replied Betsy. "I don't know yet. I have to find out how much interest will be paid for the annuity. Then, I will be able to calculate the amount we will have to pay. Does anyone else have any questions?"

Since no one else wanted to be called a twit, no other questions were asked. Once the meeting was adjourned, Betsy began contacting insurance companies and brokerage houses to check on interest rates. After continually searching, she came to the conclusion that the highest rate available for an annuity was 10%. She then began calculating the amount the city would have to spend for an annuity paying 10% interest for nine years and make it possible for the city to receive $100,000 payments each year for that period.

To calculate what the city must pay, Betsy goes down the annuity chart to the line showing nine periods, and follows the line across to 10%. The line shows the number 5.7590. That number is multiplied by one payment of $100,000. The result is $575,900, which is the price that the annuity will cost.

Since the total amount the city will have available after paying out the initial $100,000 to the winners is $900,000 and the cost of the annuity is $575,900, the city will be able to put $324,100 into the treasury. Had the annuity interest rate been 5%, it would have cost $710,780 (7.1078 x $100,000). Had the interest rate been 14%, the annuity price would have been $494,640 (4.9464 x $100.000).

After calculating the price of the annuity, Betsy calls another city council meeting to report her findings. When the council learns that the city will make $324,100, they voted to have a lottery every week. Moreover, if no one picks all five numbers on any given week, the jackpot will increase the following week.

Present Value of an Annuity (2% to 7%)

No. of Periods	2%	3%	4%	5%	6%	7%
1	0.9804	0.9709	0.9615	0.9524	0.9434	0.9346
2	1.9416	1.9135	1.8861	1.8594	1.8334	1.8080
3	2.8839	2.8286	2.7751	2.7232	2.6730	2.6243
4	3.8077	3.7171	3.6299	3.5460	3.4651	3.3872
5	4.7135	4.5797	4.4518	4.3295	4.2124	4.1002
6	5.6014	5.4172	5.2421	5.0757	4.9173	4.7665
7	6.4720	6.2303	6.0021	5.7864	5.5824	5.3893
8	7.3255	7.0197	6.7327	6.4632	6.2098	5.9713
9	8.1622	7.7861	7.4353	7.1078	6.8017	6.5152
10	8.9826	8.5302	8.1109	7.7217	7.3601	7.0236
11	9.7868	9.2526	8.7605	8.3064	7.8869	7.4987
12	10.5753	9.9540	9.3851	8.8633	8.3838	7.9427
13	11.3484	10.6350	9.9856	9.3936	8.8527	8.3577
14	12.1062	11.2961	10.5631	9.8986	9.2950	8.7455
15	12.8493	11.9379	11.1184	10.3797	9.7122	9.1079
16	13.5777	12.5611	11.6523	10.8378	10.1059	9.4466
17	14.2919	13.1661	12.1657	11.2741	10.4773	9.7632
18	14.9920	13.7535	12.6593	11.6896	10.8276	10.0591
19	15.6785	14.3238	13.1339	12.0853	11.1581	10.3356
20	16.3514	14.8775	13.5903	12.4622	11.4699	10.5940
25	19.5235	17.4131	15.6221	14.0939	12.7834	11.6536
30	22.3965	19.6004	17.2920	15.3725	13.7648	12.4090

Present Value of an Annuity (8% to 14%)

No. of Periods	8%	9%	10%	12%	14%
1	0.9259	0.9174	0.9092	0.8929	0.8772
2	1.7833	1.7591	1.7355	1.6901	1.6467
3	2.5771	2.5313	2.4869	2.4018	2.3216
4	3.3121	3.2397	3.1699	3.0373	2.9137
5	3.9927	3.8897	3.7908	3.6048	3.4331
6	4.6229	4.4859	4.3553	4.1114	3.8887
7	5.2064	5.0330	4.8684	4.5638	4.2883
8	5.7466	5.5348	5.3349	4.9676	4.6389
9	6.2469	5.9952	5.7590	5.3282	4.9464
10	6.7101	6.4177	6.1446	5.6502	5.2161
11	7.1390	6.8052	6.4951	5.9377	5.4527
12	7.5361	7.1607	6.8137	6.1944	5.6603
13	7.9038	7.4869	7.1034	6.4235	5.8424
14	8.2442	7.7862	7.3667	6.6282	6.0021
15	8.5595	8.0607	7.6061	6.8109	6.1422
16	8.8514	8.3126	7.8237	6.9740	6.2651
17	9.1216	8.5436	8.0216	7.1196	6.3729
18	9.3719	8.7556	8.2014	7.2497	6.4674
19	9.6036	8.9501	8.3649	7.3658	6.5504
20	9.8181	9.1285	8.5136	7.4694	6.6231
25	10.6748	9.8226	9.0770	7.8431	6.8729
30	11.2578	10.2737	9.4269	8.0552	7.0027

Present Value of an Annuity (15% to 24%)					
No. of Periods	**15%**	**16%**	**18%**	**20%**	**24%**
1	0.8696	0.0621	0.8475	0.8333	0.8065
2	1.6257	1.6052	1.5656	1.5278	1.4568
3	2.2832	2.2459	2.1743	2.1065	1.9813
4	2.8550	2.7982	2.6901	2.5887	2.4043
5	3.3522	3.2743	3.1272	2.9906	2.7454
6	3.7845	3.6847	3.4976	3.3255	3.0205
7	4.1604	4.0386	3.8115	3.6046	3.2423
8	4.4873	4.3436	4.0776	3.8372	3.4212
9	4.7716	4.6065	4.3030	4.0310	3.5655
10	5.0188	4.8332	4.4941	4.1925	3.6819
11	5.2337	5.0286	4.6560	4.3271	3.7757
12	5.4206	5.1971	4.7932	4.4392	3.8514
13	5.5831	5.3423	4.9095	4.5327	3.9124
14	5.7245	5.4675	5.0081	4.6106	3.9616
15	5.8474	5.5755	5.0916	4.6755	4.0013
16	5.9542	5.6685	5.1624	4.7296	4.0333
17	6.0472	5.7487	5.2223	4.7746	4.0591
18	6.1280	5.8178	5.2732	4.8122	4.0799
19	6.1982	5.8775	5.3162	4.8435	4.0967
20	6.2593	5.9288	5.3527	4.8696	4.1103
25	6.4641	6.0971	5.4669	4.9476	4.1474
30	6.5660	6.1772	5.5168	4.9789	4.1601

Appendix E
-- Synthetic Bonds

It has finally happened. For years, many of you have been wearing synthetic clothes, using synthetic furniture and eating synthetic foods. Now, you can make synthetic bonds. Synthetic Bonds are non-toxic, non-fattening and years later you won't discover that they have cancer-causing agents.

Synthetic bonds are made by mixing either zero coupon bonds or "stripped" U.S. Government treasury bonds and notes, which are offered through brokerage houses, and baking them at 350 degrees Fahrenheit. As discussed in Chapter 2, the instruments, which are called TENTS, CATS, STRIPS, etc. are stripped of their coupon payments and sold to the public at a discounted rate.

You can create your own bonds by simply buying a number of individual discounted bonds that mature on the dates you desire.

Muddy Waters wants to buy a boat and fishing tackle but does not have a lot money to spend. After going from store to store searching for a boat to fit his budget, he finally finds the boat of his dreams at Mr. Mike's Boats and Other Water Stuff.

The boat Muddy wants is being sold for $4,000. However, since it has been sitting in the showroom for twenty-six years, the dealer is anxious to sell it. As an incentive for Muddy to buy the boat, the dealer sets up a five-year payment schedule where Muddy will make a $1,000 down payment and then pay $500 per year for the first four years, and $1,000 in the fifth year.

Muddy has $4,000 in cash to pay for the boat. However, if he spends the full amount on the boat, he realizes that he will be unable to buy new fishing tackle. Moreover, since he isn't *working on a full-time basis, he doesn't want to risk the possibility of missing a payment on the boat and having it repossessed.*

Muddy discusses his problem with his cousin Soapy Waters. Soapy, who is heavy into synthetics (he was the first man ever to wear a polyester leisure suit), suggests that Muddy use a synthetic bond.

"A synthetic bond? I've never heard of a synthetic bond. I have heard of a regular bond and I know that the chances of finding a five-year bond that pays in the increments I need will be as easy as finding a nudist who doesn't play volleyball."

"A synthetic bond," replied Soapy "is not like a regular one. You make it yourself. Since you need to make payments on your boat at set intervals, all you have to do is buy five zero-coupon bonds with maturities and amounts to coincide with the payments. If you do it this way, you will be able to buy the boat, make the payments and have money left over to buy fishing tackle."

"It sounds great," stated Muddy. "Will you show me how it works?"

"Certainly," replied Soapy. Soapy begins calculating how much the bond would cost. He finds zero-coupon bonds that are paying 8% interest. Soapy creates the following chart to calculate the amount Muddy will have to spend:

Maturity	Present Value	Value at Maturity	Purchase Price
1 year	0.9259	$500.00	$462.95
2 years	0.8573	$500.00	$428.65
3 years	0.7938	$500.00	$396.90
4 years	0.7350	$500.00	$367.50
5 years	0.6806	$1,000.00	$680.60
		=======	=======
Total		$3,000.00	$2,336.60

After developing the chart, Soapy shows it to his cousin.

"I understand that the first column is the amount of years that it takes for the bond to mature," stated Muddy. "I also understand that the 'value of maturity' column is the amount that I will receive at the end of each year. I don't know what the 'present value' column is, and how you calculated the purchase price."

"The present value column," explained Soapy "is the present value of $1.00. I found those values in Appendix C of Roger's book. I multiplied the present value by the amount you will receive at maturity to calculate the price you will have to pay for the bond."

"Good gravy!!! That means that I will have $663.40 to spend on fishing tackle? That's great!!!"

By creating his own bond, Muddy will be able to save almost $700. This, of course, does not take into account the tax on the interest or the brokerage fees.

Since bonds are normally long-term instruments, setting up a situation described in the preceding example would be difficult without using a method like this. Had Muddy wanted, he could have created a scenario where he would receive $500 for the first two years, $1,000 in the third year and $500 in the last two year.

Remember, a chicken ain't nothin' but a bird and a bond ain't nothin' but an instrument with a series of payments over a period of time. Muddy simply used a number of bonds to create his own.

Appendix F
-- Talk Finance

For some time people have known how to talk tough, talk music and talk turkey. Now, with the help of this book, you will be able to do something only a chosen few were previously able to do. You will be able to TALK FINANCE. Never again will you have to cringe when the topic of a conversation shifts from "selling shoes" to "selling short." Nor will you have to leave the room when a friend asks your opinion of "day trading."

Of course, you don't have to know the terms in this appendix to make or lose money, nor do you get extra points in the game of life by calling cash "liquid assets." However, having quick access to these definitions makes it possible for you find a word like "margin," after the dictionary tells you that it is "a bordering space on a letter or page." Also, if you want to keep the romance in your marriage, say a few of these words every now and then to show your loved one that you still care. Although there are quite a few definitions listed in this section, all of the terms used in the financial world are not included. Therefore, if you don't find what you are looking for, look in another of the many publications out on the market or just do a search on the internet.

A

ACCOUNT EXECUTIVE - A person who is in direct contact with one or more of a firm's clients. The account executive handles all of the client's correspondences and transactions as they relate to the firm.

ACCRUED INTEREST - The interest that adds up on a bond since the last interest payment. The day after interest has been paid for a bond, interest begins adding up *(accruing)* every day until the next payment.

ACQUISITION - The acquiring of control of one corporation by another corporation.

AGENCY - (1) Government bonds Issued by federal entities other than the U.S. Treasury. (2) A transaction in which a broker-dealer functions as an agent *(broker)*.

ALL OR NONE (AON) - A type of order where the investor wants the entire order executed or none of it. At times, when people purchase or sell stock, they may not be able to get the total order executed.

ALPHA - A statistical measure of a stock's price volatility caused by factors other than the overall stock market.

AMERICAN DEPOSITORY RECEIPT (ADR) - A security that is issued by a U.S. bank in place of the foreign shares being held in trust by the bank. This makes it possible to trade foreign stock in the U.S. market.

AMERICAN STOCK EXCHANGE (AMEX) – *See NYSE AMEX Equities.*

ANNUITY - A series of payments of a fixed amount for a specified number of periods.

ARBITRAGE - The simultaneous purchase of securities, currency, commodities or other items in one market and sale in another market at a higher price.

ASK - *See bid and asked.*

AT THE CLOSE ORDER - An order that is supposed to be executed as close to the closing price as possible. There is never a guarantee that the execution price will be the closing price.

AT-THE-MARKET - (Also known as MARKET ORDER) An order to buy or sell a security as soon as the order reaches the floor of the exchange.

AT THE OPENING ORDER - An order to buy or sell stock at the opening price. If it is not executed at the opening, the order will be cancelled.

AUTHORIZED ISSUE - The total number of shares of capital stock that a corporation may sell.

B

BANKERS' ACCEPTANCES (BA) - A money market instrument that is used to finance international and domestic trade. BAs are checks drawn on a bank by an importer or exporter of goods and represent a bank's unconditional promise to pay the face amount of the note at maturity.

BEARER BONDS - Bonds that do not have the owner's name on the certificates and can therefore be cashed in by whoever presents them, i.e., the bearer. (These bonds should always be kept in a safe place.)

BEAR MARKET - A period in which securities prices are falling.

BETA - A statistical measure of a stock's price volatility relative to the overall stock market. If a stock's Beta is 2 and the overall market increases by 5%, the stock's price should increase by 10%. If the market decreases by 5%, the stock's price should decrease by 10%.

BID AND ASKED - The <u>bid</u> is the highest price anyone is willing to pay for a particular security at a given time and the <u>asked</u> is the lowest price anyone is willing to sell the security at the same time.

BLUE CHIP - A term used in describing a company that is well known for the quality of its services and the ability of making money and paying dividends to its stockholders.

BLUE-SKY - A term that is used to indicate whether or not a stock that is not trading on an exchange, like the New York Stock Exchange, is registered in a given state. Normally, if the company is not registered to conduct business m a state, its stock cannot be bought or sold in that state.

BONUS STOCK - Common stock that is offered as a premium.

BOND - A long-term (greater than one year) IOU from a corporation, municipality or the U.S. Government.

BOOK VALUE - In relation to stock on a per share basis, the result of the net assets divided by the total number of outstanding shares.

BREAKPOINT - The dollar level of an investment in a mutual fund at which a buyer of the fund qualifies for a reduction in sales charges.

BROKER - An agent who buys or sells stock, commodities options, etc., in return for a fee.

BULL MARKET - A period in which securities prices are rising.

C

CALL - A type of transaction in the options market that gives the buyer the right to purchase the underlying stock for a certain price within a specified period.

CALLABLE - A bond or preferred stock that can be redeemed before maturity by the issuer under specified conditions.

CAPITAL GAINS - Money made from the sale of securities or real estate. If the sale price of a security is higher than the purchase price, the difference between the two prices is the capital gain.

CAPITAL LOSSES - Money lost from the sale of securities or real estate. If the sale price of a security is lower than the purchase price, the difference between the two prices is the capital loss.

CERTIFICATE - The actual piece of paper that is evidence of ownership of a security.

CERTIFICATE OF DEPOSIT (CD) - A money market instrument issued by banks, with a set interest rate and maturity.

CLEARINGHOUSE - An organization established for the benefit and use of members of a commodity exchange to clear trades between brokers, handle adjustments of any money differences from cleared trades, provide impartial and prompt adjustments of margins between brokers, and to direct the making of deliveries on futures contracts.

CLOSE - A term used to refer to the closing prices of securities.

CLOSING TRANSACTION - The sale or purchase of an option contract to eliminate or undo an existing contract.

COMMERCIAL PAPER - A short-term (less than one year), unsecured IOU from large corporations.

COMMISSION - The broker's basic fee for buying or selling securities.

COMMON STOCK - Basic ownership class of corporate stock carrying the right to vote, sharing in earnings, participating in future stock issues and sharing in the proceeds of the corporation if it sells out all its assets.

CONVERTIBLES - Securities (normally bonds or preferred stocks) that can be exchanged, at the option of the holder, for common stock of the issuing firm.

COUPON RATE - The stated rate of interest on a bond.

CREDIT UNION SHARES - Shares in a credit union that represent ownership by its members, but is not considered securities under the Uniform Securities Act.

CYCLICAL STOCK - Stocks that are strongly affected by the business cycle.

D

DAY ORDER - An order to buy or sell a security that, if not executed, expires at the end of the trading day on which it was entered.

DAY TRADING - The act of buying and selling securities within the same day, which results m the trader not having any securities by the time the market closes.

DEBENTURE - A long-term debt instrument that is not secured by a mortgage on specific property.

DEFENSIVE STOCK - A stock that is not greatly affected by changes in the general economic activity.

DELIVERY - The physical act of exchanging securities and monies on the settlement date.

DEMAND DEPOSIT - A deposit in a bank where the depositor has the right to withdraw their money at any time (on demand) without giving prior notice to the bank.

DIRECTOR - A person elected by stockholders to serve on the Board of Directors. Directors are normally responsible for selecting the president and other corporate officers. They also decide on matters such as if and when dividends are paid.

DISCLOSURE DOCUMENT - A booklet that discusses the risk associated with option trading, which must be given to clients at or before their account is approved for options trading.

DISCOUNT RATE - The rate of interest that is charged by the Federal Reserve Bank on loans to commercial banks that are members.

DIVERSIFICATION - The act of spreading investments among different types of securities and companies.

DIVIDENDS - Distribution of a company's assets to its stockholders.

DIVIDEND REINVESTMENT - A program in which a company that pays dividends will automatically use the cash to purchase additional shares of the company.

DOLLAR COST AVERAGING - The system of buying securities at regular intervals with a fixed dollar amount. This results in buying more shares when the price is low, and less when it is high.

DOWN TICK - A term used to indicate that a transaction (e.g., stock trade) was made at a price lower than the preceding transaction.

DUAL LISTINGS - The same security listed on both the New York Stock Exchange and on a regional stock exchange.

E

EARNINGS PER SHARE (EPS) - The amount of a corporation's earnings that is available to each share of the firm's common stock.

EXCHANGE - (1) A central location where security or commodity transactions occur. (2) An offer made by a corporation to replace one type of security with another. (3) The act of switching from one mutual fund to another at little or no cost.

EXERCISE PRICE - The price that the underlying security in an option contract can be bought (called) or sold (put).

EXPIRATION DATE - The latest date that an option can be exercised.

F

FACE VALUE - The value of a bond that appears on the bond's face, which is normally the amount that an investor will receive when the instrument matures.

FAMILY OF FUNDS - A group of mutual funds managed by the same investment company.

FANNIE MAE - *See Federal National Mortgage Association.*

FEDERAL FARM CREDIT SYSTEM - A group of government agencies that extend credit to farmers.

FEDERAL FINANCING BANK (FFB) – An entity authorized to acquire any note, bond or other obligation that is issued or guaranteed by a federal agency, with the exception of the Federal Farm Credit System, the Federal Home Loan Mortgage Corporation and the Federal National Mortgage Corporation.

FEDERAL FUNDS (FED FUNDS) - (1) The overnight borrowing of reserves by a bank from another bank. (2) Funds that is immediately available.

FED FUNDS RATE - The interest rate that banks charge each other on overnight loans of reserves held at the FFB.

FEDERAL HOME LOAN BANKS (FHLB) - An entity that operates as a credit reserve system for savings-related institutions in the U.S.

FEDERAL HOME LOAN MORTGAGE CORPORATION (FHLMC) - *Also called Freddie Mac.* Provides a secondary market for conventional residential mortgages and issues a number of mortgage backed securities.

FEDERAL HOUSING ADMINISTRATION (FHA) - Federal agency that insures lenders against defaults on residential mortgages.

FEDERAL INTERMEDIATE CREDIT BANKS (FICB) – A part of the Federal Farm Credit System, it provides intermediate-term loans for agricultural purposes.

FEDERAL LAND BANK (FLB) - A part of the Federal Farm Credit System that provides long-term loans to farmers and ranchers for various agricultural purposes.

FEDERAL NATIONAL MORTGAGE ASSOCIATION (FNMA) - *Also called Fannie Mae.* A privately owned corporation that provides a secondary market for federally guaranteed or insured mortgages as well as conventional mortgages.

FEDERAL OPEN MARKET COMMITTEE (FOMC) - A committee of the Federal Reserve Board that operates by buying and selling government securities in the open market.

FEDERAL RESERVE BOARD - The governmental entity responsible for the United States monetary policy.

FILL-OR-KILL (FOK) - Instructions to immediately execute a transaction in its entirety or cancel it.

FINANCIAL FUTURES - Futures contracts that are based on financial instruments such as Treasury bonds, certificates of deposit, foreign currencies and stock market indicators.

FINRA - Financial Industry Regulatory Authority, Inc. is a private corporation that acts as a self-regulatory organization (SRO). FINRA is the successor to the National Association of Securities Dealers, Inc. (NASD). It is not part of the U.S. government and is not a government agency. FINRA is a private corporation that performs market regulation under contract with brokerage firms and trading markets.

FIXED ANNUITY - An annuity contract in which an insurance company makes fixed dollar payments to the annuitant for the term of the contract.

FLOOR - The trading area where stocks and bonds are bought and sold on an exchange.

FREDDIE MAC - *See Federal Home Loan Mortgage Corporation.*

FUNDAMENTAL RESEARCH - The analysis of industries and companies based on factors such as sales, assets, earnings, products or services, markets and management.

FUTURES - Contracts traded on an exchange that specifies a future date of delivery or receipt of a certain amount of a specific tangible or intangible product.

G

GENERAL OBLIGATION BOND (GO) - A municipal bond secured by the issuer having the ability to tax individuals or businesses in the municipality.

GINNIE MAE - *See Government National Mortgage Association.*

GOOD-TIL-CANCELLED ORDER (GTC) - An order to buy or sell a security that remains in effect until it is either executed or cancelled.

GOING PUBLIC - An occurrence whereby a private corporation, one owned by a small group of individuals, issues shares of its stock to be traded on the open market.

GOVERNMENT BONDS - Bonds issued by the U.S. Government and regarded as the highest grade of securities issued.

GOVERNMENT NATIONAL MORTGAGE ASSOCIATION (GNMA) - *Also called Ginnie Mae.* A wholly owned government corporation that help raise funds for the mortgage market by guaranteeing securities backed by pools of mortgages.

GROWTH STOCK - Stock of a company with a record of rapid growth of earnings.

H

HOLDER - The buyer of owner of a security.

HOLDING COMPANY - A corporation operating for the purpose of owning the common stocks of other corporations.

HOLDING PERIOD - The time period that an investor has owned a security.

HYPOTHECATION - The pledging of securities as collateral.

I

IMMEDIATE-OR-CANCEL ORDER (IOC) - An order where as much of the order as possible must be executed immediately and any part of the order that is not executed is cancelled.

INCOME FUND - A type of mutual fund consisting of a portfolio of income producing securities such as bonds and preferred stock.

INCOME STOCK - A stock that pays a relatively high dividend.

INDENTURE - A formal agreement between the issuer of a bond and the bondholder, which sets forth the maturity date, interest rate and other terms.

INDEX FUND - A mutual fund with a goal to grow at the same level as the general market.

INDEX OPTION - Options contracts that are traded on an underlying index rather than a particular security.

INITIAL PUBLIC OFFERING (IPO) - The first public issue of stock from a company that has not previously been traded publicly.

INSURED BONDS - Municipal bonds that are covered by an insurance policy that pledges that the insurance company will pay all interest and principal due if the issuer fails to make a payment.

INTEREST - Payments made by a borrower to a lender for the use of the lender's money.

INTEREST RATE OPTIONS - Options contracts traded on underlying debt instruments.

INTEREST RATE RISK - The risk that an investment in a fixed income security will decrease in value.

INTERMEDIATION - The placement of money with financial intermediaries such as banks and insurance companies, which in turn invests in stocks, bonds or mortgages.

IN-THE-MONEY - An option with intrinsic value.

INTRINSIC VALUE - The amount that the market price of a stock is above the strike price of a call option or below the strike price of a put option on that stock.

INVESTMENT - The use of money for the purpose of making more money.

INVESTMENT BANKER - A person who underwrites and distributes new investment securities.

INVESTMENT COMPANY - A company or trust engaged in the business of investing in securities.

INVESTMENT GRADE - Refers to bonds rated in the top four rating categories by Moody's or Standard & Poor's.

ISSUE - Any of a company's securities or the act of distributing the securities.

ISSUER - The organizations issuing or proposing to issue a security.

L

LEVERAGED BUYOUT (LBO) - The act of taking over a company using borrowed funds.

LIMIT, LIMITED ORDER OR LIMITED PRICE ORDER - An order to buy or sell a stated amount of a security at a specified price or better.

LIMITED TAX BOND - A municipal bond that is secured by a pledge of taxes, but limited as to the rate or amount.

LISTED STOCK - The stock of a company that is traded on an exchange.

LOAD - The portion of a mutual fund's offering price in excess of the net asset value, which covers sales commissions and all other costs of distribution.

M

MANAGEMENT COMPANY - A type of investment company organized as a corporation that actively manages the portfolio of securities held by the investment company.

MANAGEMENT FEE - The expense paid by an investment company to the investment advisor for managing the portfolio.

MARGIN - The percentage of the cost of a stock, commodity or other security that is paid by the buyer.

MARGIN CALL - A demand, to a securities holder from a broker, that more cash or more collateral be placed into the holder's account.

MARKET ORDER - An order to buy or sell a stated amount of a security at the best price possible after the order is entered.

MARKET PRICE - The last reported price at which a stock or bond was sold, or the current quote.

MARKET RISK - The risk that the value of a security will decline in price.

MATURITY - The date that a loan or bond comes due and is to be paid off.

MERGER - The combination of two or more corporations for the purpose of making operations more efficient.

MONEY MARKET - Financial markets in which funds are borrowed or lent for short periods of time (less than one year).

MONEY MARKET FUND - A mutual fund investing in money market instruments.

MUNICIPAL BOND - A bond issued by a state or political subdivision such as a county, city or school district.

MUTUAL FUND - A type of investment company that offers securities that are redeemable on demand by the fund at the current net asset value.

N

NASD - The National Association of Securities Dealers. *(See FINRA)*

NASDAQ - The National Association of Securities Dealers Automated Quotations, which is an automated information network that provides brokers and dealers with price quotations on securities traded over-the-counter.

NET ASSET VALUE (NAV) - The value of a single share of a mutual fund.

NET CHANGE - The change in the price of a security from the closing price from the previous day.

NEW ISSUE - A security sold by an issuer for the first time.

NEW YORK FUTURES EXCHANGE (NYFE) - A subsidiary of the New York Stock Exchange that is devoted to the trading of financial futures contracts.

NEW YORK STOCK EXCHANGE (NYSE) - The largest organized securities market in the United States.

NO LOAD FUND - A mutual fund that charges no sales charge on the purchase of shares.

NON-COMPETITIVE TENDER - A method that a small investor can use to purchase Treasury bills at the original auction.

NON-CUMULATIVE - A type of preferred stock where unpaid dividends do not accrue and normally gone forever.

NYSE AMEX EQUITIES - Formerly known as the American Stock Exchange (AMEX), it is the second largest stock exchange in the United States.

NYSE COMMON STOCK INDEX – A composite index that covers the price movements of all common stocks listed on the New York Stock Exchange.

O

ODD LOT - An amount of stock that is less than the established unit of trading, which is normally 100 shares.

ODD LOT THEORY - An investment strategy that assumes that the small investor is always wrong.

OFFER - The price at which and investor is ready to sell a security.

OPEN - END INVESTMENT COMPANY - *See Investment Company.*

OPENING TRANSACTION - The purchase or sale of an option transaction to establish a position.

OPEN MARKET COMMITTEE - *See Federal Open Market Committee.*

OPEN ORDER - *See Good Til Cancelled Order.*

OPTIONS - Contracts that give their holder the right to buy or sell an asset at a predetermined time for a given period of time.

OTC MARKETS – Formerly known as the Pink Sheets, it is an electronic trading platform where investors can buy and sell stock issued by small public companies, foreign companies and companies that are not listed on other stock exchanges.

OUT-OF-THE-MONEY - An option that has no intrinsic value.

OUTSTANDING STOCK - The amount of a corporation's stock that is owned by investors.

OVER-THE-COUNTER MARKET (OTC) - All facilities that provide for trading in securities not listed on organized exchanges.

P

PASSED DIVIDEND - A regular or scheduled dividend that is not paid out to investors.

PAPER DEALER - A securities dealer specializing in buying and selling commercial paper.

PAPER PROFIT (LOSS) - The profit or loss on a security still being held by investors. Actual profits and losses occur and are taxable only when the security is sold.

PAR - (1) The face value or principal value of a bond. (2) The face value of a preferred stock on which book value, liquidating value and dividend payments is based. (3) The stated value of common stock used primarily for bookkeeping purposes. It has no relationship to market value.

PARTICIPATING PREFERRED STOCK - A preferred stock in which the holder is entitled to its stated dividend and to additional dividends on a specified basis after payment of dividends on the common stock has been made.

PARTNERSHIP - An entity in which each partner shares in the profits, losses and liabilities. Each partner is responsible for the taxes on its share of profits and losses. *See Limited Partnership.*

PENNY STOCKS - Low-priced stocks selling for less than $5 a share.

PERIOD CERTAIN - An annuity policy that guarantees a minimum number of annuity payments to the annuitant (or beneficiaries).

PINK SHEETS – *See OTC Markets.* A daily publication that provides quotes for over-the-counter stocks.

POINT - In the case of shares of stock, a point means $1. *(For example, if IBM stock rises 5 points, each share has increased by $5.)* In the case of bonds, a point means $10 because bonds are quoted as a percentage of $1,000. *(For example, a bond that rises 5 points increases 5% of $1,000, or $50 in value.)* In the case of market averages, the word point means merely that, and nothing else. *(If, for example, the Dow Jones Industrial average rises from 7880.52 to 7885.52, it has risen 5 points.)* However, a point in this average is not equivalent to $1.

PORTFOLIO - The holdings of securities by an individual or institution, which might consist of bonds, preferred stocks, common stocks and other securities.

PORTFOLIO INCOME – A category of income consisting of dividends, interest and capital gains.

POSITION - An individual's stake in a financial market.

POSITION LIMIT - The limitation established by the option exchanges that prohibits an investor from having a position of more than an established number of option contracts of the same security on the same side of the market.

PREFERRED STOCK - (1) A class of stock that is usually entitled to dividends at a specified rate when declared by the Board of Directors and before payment of a dividend on the common stock.

PRELIMINARY PROSPECTUS - *See Red Herring.*

PREMIUM - (1) A bond trading in the market above its face value. (2) The amount a bond's current price exceeds its face value. (3) The amount a bond's redemption price exceeds its face value, which is known as the "call premium". (4) The market price of an option contract set by supply and demand.

PREPAYMENT RISK - The risk that, due to falling interest rates, mortgage holders will pay off their mortgages at a faster than expected rate, which will result in investors not receiving all of the interest they expect.

PRESENT VALUE (PV) - The value today of a future payment discounted at the appropriate discount rate.

PRICE-EARNINGS RATIO *(P/E)* - The price of a share of stock, divided by earnings per share for a twelve-month period. *(For example, if a stock is selling for $50 per share and earning $5 per share, it is selling at a price-earnings ratio of 10.)*

PRICE SPREAD - An option spread position in which the strike prices of the options are different, but the expiration dates are the same. Also called a Vertical or Money Spread.

PRIMARY MARKET - The market for new issues or underwritings.

PRIME RATE - The lowest interest rate charged by commercial banks to their most creditworthy and largest corporate customers.

PRINCIPAL - (1) The face value or par value of a debt instrument. (2) The amount of money that a person has invested.

PRIVATE ACTIVITY BONDS - A type of municipal bonds where the interest earned may or may not be subject to federal income tax.

PRIVATE PLACEMENT - *See Regulation D Offering.*

PROFIT-TAKING - Selling stock that has increased in value since purchase in order to realize the profit.

PROSPECTUS - The official selling circular that must be given to investors who purchase new securities registered with the Securities and Exchange Commission. It discusses key elements of the Registration Statement filed with the Commission, which is much longer. The prospectus warns that the stock being issued has not been approved or disapproved by the Commission and discloses information such as the property and business of the company issuing the stock, the nature of the security offered, use of proceeds, company's competition and prospects, management's experience, history, and remuneration and certified financial statements.

PROXY - Written permission given by a shareholder that authorizes someone else to represent him and vote his shares at a shareholders' meeting.

PROXY FIGHT - The attempt between opposing parties to secure the proxy of shareholders.

PROXY STATEMENT - Information given to stockholders in conjunction with the request of proxies.

PUBLIC OFFERING - The original sale of a company's securities.

PURCHASING POWER RISK - The risk that, because of inflation, the money returned from an investment will not be worth as much as the original amount invested.

PUT BOND - A bond that can be redeemed at the holder's option on a specific date or dates.

PUT - A type of transaction in the options market that gives a buyer the right to sell the underlying stock for a certain price within a designated period.

Q

QUOTE - The highest bid to buy and the lowest offer to sell a security in a given market at a given time.

R

RALLY - A rapid rise following a decline in the general price level of the market or an individual stock.

RANDOM WALK - A theory that assumes that future price movements of a security cannot be predicted from past price movements, which refutes technical analysts' use of charts as a method of forecasting stock prices. Basically, the theory argues that prices move in a random pattern and are no more predictable than the walking pattern of a drunken person.

RATING - The evaluation of credit risk of securities by an established rating service such as Moody's or Standard & Poor's.

REAL ESTATE INVESTMENT TRUST (REIT) - An organization, similar to an investment company, which concentrates its holdings in real estate investments. The yield is generally good because REITs are required to distribute as much as 95% of their income to investors.

RECORD DATE - The date on which you must be registered as a shareholder of a company in order to receive a declared dividend or, among other things, to vote on company affairs.

REDEMPTION - (1) Repayment of a debt security at or before maturity. (2) Repayment of a preferred stock. (3) Sale of mutual fund shares to the fund sponsor.

RED HERRING - A preliminary version of the prospectus that is used by brokers to determine if potential investors might be interested in purchasing the security. It is called "red herring" because of a front-page notice (printed in red ink) that the preliminary prospectus is "subject to completion or amendment" and "shall not constitute an offer to sell."

REFUNDING BOND - Issuing a new bond issue for the purpose of retiring an outstanding bond issue.

REGISTERED - (1) A certificate in which the name of the owner is recorded on the books of the issuer. It can be transferred only when endorsed by the registered owner.

REGULAR WAY DELIVERY - The normal industry standard for handling the sale and purchase of securities. Unless otherwise specified, most securities sold are to be delivered to the buying broker by the selling broker and payment made to the selling broker by the buying broker on the third business day after the transaction. Regular way delivery for government securities and options is the following business day.

REGULATION A OFFERING - A type of new issue that is partially exempt from the filing requirements of the Securities Act of 1933. The exemption is given if the issue is a no more than $5,000,000.

REGULATION D OFFERING - *Also called a Private Placement.* A type of issue that is sold directly to investors by the issuer instead of through underwriters. Although the size of the issue is not limited, its sale is limited to a maximum of thirty-five non-accredited investors.

REINVESTMENT RISK - The risk that bond investors who choose to spend the interest or is unable to reinvest the coupon payments, will not receive the calculated yield to maturity.

RESISTANCE- The upper range of an established trading range where selling pressure tends to cause the price of a stock to decline (versus Support).

REPURCHASE AGREEMENT (REPO or RP) – A transaction whereby the Federal Open Market Committee buys securities such as T-bills from a non-bank dealer and the non-bank dealer agrees to repurchase them a short time later at a predetermined price.

RESTRICTED STOCK - Stock that is not registered under the Securities Act of 1933. Stock purchased through a company's stock option plan or a private placement will be unregistered. The holding period for restricted stock is up to two years.

RETAINED EARNINGS - The profits that a corporation does not pay out in dividends and are kept by the company to help finance expansion.

RETIREMENT - Repayment of debt obligations such as bonds.

REVENUE ANTICIPATION NOTE (RAN) - A short-term municipal security used by a municipality to help its cash flow. RANs have a maximum maturity of one year and repayment is based on certain anticipated revenues of the municipality.

REVENUE BOND - A bond issue that is secured by a pledge of the revenues of a specific project.

REVERSE REPO - The opposite of a Repurchase Agreement.

REVERSE STOCK SPLIT - An action companies use to decrease the number of shares of stock on the market without buying the existing shares. *(For example, a four-for-one reverse split would mean that a person who began owning 4 shares of stock would end up with 1 share. However, if the original shares were worth $1.00 each, the new one would be worth $4.00.)*

RIGHTS - When a company wants to raise more money by issuing additional securities, it may give its stockholders the opportunity, ahead of others, to buy the new securities in proportion to the number of shares each owns. The piece of paper indicating that an investor has this privilege is called a right.

RIGHTS OF ACCUMULATION - The ability of "related" mutual fund investors to pool their combined purchases to meet break points.

RISK - The chance that an investor has of losing all or part of an investment.

ROUND LOT - A unit of trading or a multiple thereof. On the most exchanges, the unit of trading is 100 shares in stocks and $1,000 or $5,000 par value m the case of bonds.

RULE 144 - This allows owners to sell restricted stock or control stock. Filing with the SEC is required prior to selling restricted and control stock and the number of shares that may be sold is limited.

S

SALES CHARGE - The amount of the purchase price of mutual fund shares that an underwriter will receive and, therefore, not be invested in shares.

SALLIE MAE - *See Student Loan Marketing Association.*

SAME SIDE OF THE MARKET - Relates to an option investor's expectations for the underlying security. Selling calls and buying puts are one side of the market and buying calls and selling puts are the other.

SCRIP CERTIFICATE - A fractional share of a stock issued by a corporation.

SEASONAL STOCK - A company whose earnings and sales vary because of weather, holidays, etc. *(An example is a toy manufacturer with heavy sales during Christmas.)*

SEAT - A figure-of-speech for an individual or company being a member of an exchange.

SECONDARY MARKET - The trading of existing or outstanding securities (vs. new issues) that occur on exchanges or over the counter.

SECURED BOND - A corporate bond that has an asset pledged as collateral.

SECURITIES ACT OF 1933 - The federal law that covers how securities are to be reported to the public. It requires full-disclosure of pertinent information relating to the new issue and contains anti-fraud provisions.

SECURITIES AND EXCHANGE COMMISSION (SEC) – The Securities and Exchange Commission, which was established by Congress to help protect investors. The SEC administers the Securities Act of 1933, the Securities Exchange Act of 1934, the Securities Act Amendments of 1975, the Trust Indenture Act, the Investment Company Act, the Investment Advisers Act and the Public Utility Holding Company Act.

SECURITIES EXCHANGE ACT OF 1934 - The federal law that regulates broker-dealers and secondary market securities transactions.

SECURITIES INVESTOR PROTECTION CORPORATION (SIPC) – A nonprofit membership corporation composed of all brokers and dealers registered under the Securities Exchange Act of 1934, all members of national securities exchanges and most NASD members. SIPC provides customers of these firms protection of up to $500,000 of coverage for their cash and securities held by the firm.

SECURITY - Any document such as stocks, bonds or notes. Insurance or endowment policies, credit union shares and fixed annuities are not considered securities.

SELLER'S OPTION - A special transaction giving the seller the right to deliver the stock or bond at any time within a specified period, which ranges from not less than two business days to no time limit at all.

SEPARATE ACCOUNT - Used with a variable annuity, investors' payments to an insurance company are invested in securities that are kept separate from the insurer's general investments.

SERIES OF OPTION - A complete description of an option contract, which includes the name of the underlying security, the contract size, expiration date and strike price.

SETTLEMENT - A securities transaction where a broker-dealer pays for securities purchased or delivers securities sold and receives the proceeds of the sale. Regular way settlement for most securities is three business days from trade date. Government bonds and options settle the next business day. A transaction done for cash settles on the same day.

SHORT POSITION - The amount of stock that an individual has sold short and has not covered, as of a particular date.

SHORT SELLING - Selling a security that is not owned by the seller at the time of the sale. The seller borrows the security from a broker and must repay the broker by buying the security on the open market.

SHORT SWING PROFIT - Profits made on stock held less than six months.

SKIP DAY - Settlement for U.S. Government bond trades that occurs 2 business days after trade date (vs. Regular Way).

SPECIALIZED FUND - A type of mutual fund whose portfolio consists of stocks in a specific industry or geographical area.

SPECIAL TAX BOND - A municipal bond that is secured by a pledge of a specific special tax. It is not a general obligation since it is limited to one specific tax.

SPECULATION - The use of funds by a speculator whose primary concern is for high return on investment and safety of principal being a secondary factor.

SPECULATOR – A person who is willing to assume a relatively large risk in the hope of a large gain.

SPOT PRICE - The price that an investor will have to pay for a security or commodity at the lime it is quoted.

SPREAD - The difference between the "bid" and "asked" price of a security or commodity.

STANDARD AND POOR'S (S&P) - A company that publishes a variety of resource materials relating to securities and has a rating service for both municipal and corporate securities.

STANDARD & POOR'S 500 INDEX (S&P 500) – A composite index consisting of 500 stocks.

STOCK DIVIDEND - A dividend paid in additional shares of stock rather than in cash.

STOCK EXCHANGE - *See Exchange.*

STOCKHOLDER - The owner of common or preferred stock, which signifies an ownership interest (equity) in a corporation.

STOCKHOLDER OF RECORD - A stockholder whose name is registered on the books of the issuing corporation.

STOCK SPLIT - An action companies use to increase the number of shares of stock on the market without issuing new shares. *(For example, a four-for-one split would mean that a person who started off with one share of stock would end up with four. However, if the original share was worth $1.00, the new ones would be worth 25¢ each.)*

STOP-LIMIT ORDER - An order to a broker that gives a price above which the item can't be bought and below which it can't be sold.

STOP-LOSS ORDER - An order given to a broker to buy or sell a security or commodity if it reaches a certain price to limit loss or protect profit on an existing purchase.

STRADDLE - An option position in which an investor purchases or sells a call option and a put option on the same underlying stock. The expiration month and exercise price of each contract must be the same.

STRIKE PRICE - Also known as the exercise price, it is the price at which the option buyer may purchase the stock.

STRIP - A brokerage house practice of separating a bond into its face and coupons, which are then sold separately as zero coupon bonds. Stripped U.S. Government bonds are generally referred to as "Treasury Receipts", but are better known as CATS, STRIPS, etc.

STUDENT LOAN MARKETING ASSOCIATION (SLMA) – A private, for-profit corporation, also known as Sallie Mae, that provides a secondary market for insured student loans made under the Guaranteed Student Loan Program.

SUBSCRIPTION - The purchase of stock under the terms of a right or warrant at the subscription price that may be higher or lower than the market price.

SUBSCRIPTION AGREEMENT - The application submitted by an investor wishing to join a limited partnership.

SUITABILITY - An investment that meets an investor's investment objectives and financial situation.

SUPPORT - The lower trading price of an established trading range where buying pressure tends to bid up the price of the stock (vs. resistance).

SWAPPING - The act of selling securities that are owned, and almost simultaneously purchasing different securities. Stock swaps are often done to establish losses for tax purposes (tax-swap) and bond swaps may be done to increase income, alter maturity and/or upgrade quality.

T

TAPE - *See Ticker*.

TAXABLE EQUIVALENT YIELD - An adjustment made to a tax-free yield so investors can compare them to taxable yields.

TAX ANTICIPATION NOTE (TAN) – A short-term municipal security with a maximum maturity of one year and repayment based on specific future tax collections of the municipality.

TECHNICAL RESEARCH - The technical study of price movements, volume, and trends and patterns by charting these factors to determine how future prices will move.

TENDER - (1) The act of surrendering securities in response to an offer to buy them at a set price. (2) To submit a bid to buy a security.

TENDER OFFER - A public offer to buy shares from existing stockholders of one public corporation by another firm or organization under specified terms that are good for a certain time period. Stockholders are asked to "tender" (surrender) their stock for a stated value, which is usually higher than the current market price, and subject to the tendering of a minimum and maximum number of shares.

THIRD MARKET- Trading a stock that is listed on an exchange in the over-the-counter market by non-exchange member brokers.

TICKER - The telegraphic system, which is also known as the "tape," that prints or displays last sale prices and volume of securities transactions on exchanges on a moving tape within a minute after each trade.

TIME DEPOSIT - Deposits where the depositor agrees to leave the money in for a set period of time, and is not available on demand.

TIME VALUE - The amount of an options premium that exceeds the intrinsic value of an options contract.

TIP - Supposedly "inside" information on a corporation's affairs that might give investors a trading advantage.

TRADE DATE - The day on which the actual purchase or sale of a
security is made.

TRANSFER - (1) The delivery of a stock certificate from the seller's
broker to the buyer's broker and the legal change of ownership. (2)
To record the change of ownership on the books of the corporation
by the transfer agent. Once the purchaser's name is recorded,
dividends, notices of meetings, proxies, financial reports and all
related information sent by the issuer to its securities holders is
mailed to the new owner.

TRANSFER AGENT - The entity that keeps a record of the name and
address of each registered shareholder, the number of shares owned
and assures that certificates presented to the office for transfer are
properly canceled and new certificates are issued in the name of the
new owner.

TREASURY BILLS (T-BILLS) - Short-term U.S. Government
obligations. They are purchased at a discount and mature at the face
value.

TREASURY BONDS - U.S. Government securities with original
maturities of more than ten years. Interest is normally paid twice a
year.

TREASURY NOTES - U.S. Government securities with original
maturities between one year and ten years. Interest is normally paid
twice a year.

TREASURY STOCK - Stock that a corporation originally sold to the
public, but later repurchased.

TRIPLE TAX EXEMPT - Municipal bonds in which the bondholder
pays no federal, state or local taxes on the interest. These are
typically issued by possessions and territories of the U.S., such as
Guam, Puerto Rico and the U.S. Virgin Islands.

U

UNDERLYING SECURITY - The stock for which an option was
purchased or sold.

UNDERWRITING - The process of issuing new corporate securities.

UN-ISSUED STOCK - Stock that a corporation has the authority to sell
to the public, but has not done so.

UNIFORM GIFT TO MINORS ACT (UGMA) - The act that establishes rules governing the purchase of securities for a minor. A gift to a minor cannot be taken away from the minor and securities must be registered in the name of an adult who functions as custodian for the minor.

UNIT INVESTMENT TRUST (UIT) - A type of investment where an investment company purchases a portfolio of financial instruments and it is held for a set amount of time with little or no change to the investments.

UNLISTED SECURITIES - Securities that are traded in the over-the-counter market or the OTC Markets (Pink Sheets).

UPTICK - A term used to indicate that a transaction (e.g., stock trade) was made at a price higher than the preceding transaction.

V

VARIABLE ANNUITY - A life insurance annuity contract where the annuity premium (a set dollar amount) is immediately turned into units of a portfolio of stocks. After retirement, the policyholder is paid according to the accumulated units whose dollar value varies according to the performance of the stock portfolio.

VOLATILITY - Price fluctuation.

W

WARRANT - A long-term option to buy a stated number of shares of stock at a specified price.

WIRE HOUSE - A brokerage firm with a network of branch offices that are linked together by various communications devices.

WRITER - The person who sells options to an individual or organization. The writer, however, should not be confused with the broker. The broker, as in the other markets, is the one that executes the transactions.

Y

YIELD - The rate of return on an investment.

YIELD-TO-CALL (YTC) - The rate of return an investor earns from a bond, assuming that the bond is redeemed (called) before the maturity date.

YIELD-TO-MATURITY (YTM) - The rate of return an investor earns from a bond if the bond is held to the maturity date.

Z

ZERO-COUPON BOND - A bond that is sold at a price lower than the face value and does not pay interest on a periodic basis. Instead, it pays the face value at maturity.

Appendix G
-- Directory of Publications

There are so many books on investing that it would be impossible and impractical to try listing all of them. Also, the internet provides a plethora of information, both good and bad, about investing. The following lists are comprised of publications that might be helpful if you wish to delve more deeply into the wonderful world of investing. A lot of the books listed were written a number of years ago. I made a point to include those publications because there is not a big difference between investing then and now. Moreover, I have found the older publications to be a bit more informative.

Public libraries have some of the books on the list, as well as many not included. I strongly recommend that you do not get bogged down in literature. Try to get an idea of what you are looking for and then check the library, book store and the internet to see what they have on the subject. Remember two things:

- Some books are written on strategy, while others involve in-depth explanations of the instruments. Decide which one is best for you.

- Most authors do not become wealthy following their advice; they make money by selling you a book, which means that you should not follow anyone's suggestions blindly (except mine).

Bonds

Darst, David M., *The Handbook of the Bond and Money Markets*, (New York: McGraw Hill, 1981).

The European Bond Markets: An Overview and Analysis for Issuers and Investors, the European Bond Commission, (Chicago, IL: Probus Pub. Co., 1989).

Fabozzi, Frank J., *Bond Markets, Analysis and Strategies,* 3rd ed. (Upper Saddle River, NJ: Prentice Hall, 1996).

The Global Bond Markets: State-Of-The-Art Research, Analysis and Investment Strategies, Jess Lederman. Keith K.H. Park, editors, (Chicago, IL: Probus Pub. Co., 1991).

Grabbe. J. Orlin, *International Financial Markets,* 3rd ed., (Englewood Cliffs, NJ: Prentice Hall, 1996).

How The Bond Market Works, Staff of New York Institute of Finance, (New York, NY: New York Institute of Finance, 1988).

The New High Yield Bond Market: Investment Opportunities, Strategies and Analysis. Jess Lederman. Michael P. Sullivan. [editors], (Chicago. IL: Probus Pub. Co., 1993).

Partridge-Hicks, Stephen, *Synthetic Securities,* (London: Euromoney Publications, 1988).

Ray, Christina I., *The Bond Market: Trading And Risk Management.* (Homewood, IL: Business One Irwin, 1993).

Walmsley, Julian, *Global Investing: Eurobonds and Alternatives.* (New York: St. Martin's Press, 1991).

Wilson, Richard S., *The New Corporate Bond Market: A Complete and Insightful Analysis Of The Latest Trends, Issues and Advances*, (Chicago, IL: Probus Publishing Co., 1990).

Commodities

Blume, Marshall E. and Jack P. Friedman, eds., *Encyclopedia of Investments,* (Boston: Warren, Gorham & Lamont, 1982).

Chicago Mercantile Exchange, *Trading in Tomorrows: Your Guide to Futures,* (Chicago: Chicago Mercantile Exchange, 1982).

Hieronymus, Thomas A., *Economics of Futures Trading: For Commercial and Personal Profit,* 2nd ed., (New York: Commodity Research Bureau, Inc., 1980).

Huff, Charles and Barbara Marinacci, *Commodity Speculation for Beginners: A Guide to the Futures Market*, (New York: Macmillan, 1980).

Margins & Market Integrity: State Of The Art Research On The Impact Of Margins In Stocks and Futures Markets, Mid America Institute, (Chicago, IL: Probus Publishing Co., 1991).

Powers, Mark J., *Getting Started in Commodity Futures Trading,* 3rd ed., (Cedar Falls, Iowa: Investor Publications, Inc., 1983).

Teweles, Richard J., Charles V. Harlow and Herbert L. Stone, *The Commodity Futures Game: Who Wins? Who Loses? Why?,* Abridged Ed., (New York: McGraw Hill, 1977).

Foreign Currency

Kaufman, Perry J., *Handbook of Futures Markets: Commodity, Financial. Stock Index. Options*, (New York: Wiley, 1984).

Rothstein, Nancy H. and James M. Little, eds., *The Handbook of Financial Futures: A Guide for Investors and Professional Financial Managers*, (New York: McGraw Hill, 1984).

Money Market Funds

Donoghue, William E. (with Thomas Tilling), *William E. Donoghue's Complete Money Market Guide,* (New York: Harper and Row, 1980).

Stigum, Marcia, *The Money Market,* Rev. ed., (Homewood, IL: Dow Jones-Irwin, 1983).

The Handbook of Fixed Income Securities, Frank J. Fabozzi, editor, and T. Dessa Fabozzi, editor, 4th ed., (Burr Ridge, IL: Irwin Professional Publications, 1995).

Sullivan, Colleen, *The Money Market Fund Primer,* (New York: Macmillan, 1983).

Wann, Peter, *Inside the US Treasury Market,* (New York: Woodhead-Faulkner, 1989).

Mutual Funds

Bogle, John C., *Bogle on Mutual Funds: New Perspectives for the Intelligent Investor*, (Burr Ridge, IL: Business One Irwin, 1994).

Boroson, Warren, *Keys to Investing in Mutual Funds,* 2nd ed., (New York: Barron's, 1992).

Brouwer, Kurt, *Kurt Brouwer's Guide to Mutual Funds: How to Invest with the Pros*, (New York: Wiley, 1990).

Hirsch, Michael D., *The Mutual Fund Wealth Builder: A mutual fund strategy that won't let you down no matter what the market is doing,* (New York: Harper Business, 1991).

How To Succeed at Mutual Fund Investing [video recording], (Seattle, WA: Paul Merriman & Associates, 1994).

Lavine, Alan, *50 Ways to Mutual Fund Profits,* (Chicago: Irwin, 1996).

Mutual Funds. Options and Commodities, [video recording]: *An Investment Primer,* (Alexandria, VA: PBS Home Video; Los Angeles: Pacific Arts Video, 1991).

Perritt, Gerald W., *Mutual Funds Made Easy,* (Chicago: Dearborn Financial Publications, 1995).

Rugg, Donald D. and Norman B. Hale. *The Dow Jones-Irwin Guide to Mutual Funds,* Rev. ed., (Homewood, IL: Dow Jones-Irwin, 1983).

Vince, Ralph, *Portfolio Management Formulas: Mathematical trading methods for the futures, options and stock markets,* (New York: Wiley, 1990).

Vujovich, Dian, *Straight Talk About Mutual Funds,* (New York: McGraw-Hill, 1992).

Options

Apostolou, Nicholas G., *Keys to Investing in Options and Futures,* (New York: Barron's, 1991).

Clasing, Henry K. Jr., *The Dow Jones-Irwin Guide to Put & Call Options,* Rev. ed., (Homewood, IL: Dow Jones-Irwin, 1978).

Fabozzi, Frank J. and Frank G. Zarb, eds., *Handbook of Financial Markets: Securities, Options, Futures,* (Homewood, IL: Dow Jones Irwin, 1981).

Gastineau, Gary L., *The Stock Options Manual,* 2nd ed., (New York: McGraw Hill, 1979).

McMillan, Lawrence G., *Options as a Strategic Investment: A Comprehensive Analysis of Listed Option Strategies*, (New York: New York Institute of Finance, 1980).

Sarnoff, Paul, *Puts and Calls: The Complete Guide*, (Hawthorn, 1968).

Stark. Brian J., *Special Situation Investing: Hedging, Arbitrage and Liquidation*, (Homewood, IL: Dow Jones-Irwin, 1983).

Van Peebles, Melvin. *Bold Money: A New Way to Play the Options Market,* (New York, NY: Warner Books, 1986).

Stocks

Case, Samuel, *Big Profits From Small Stocks: How to grow your investment portfolio by investing in small cap companies*, (Rocklin, CA: Prima Publications, 1995).

Engel, Louis and Brendan Boyd, *How to Buy Stocks,* 7th rev. ed., (Boston: Little, Brown, 1982).

Graham, Benjamin, David L. Dodd and Sidney Cottle, *Security Analysis: Principles and Techniques,* 4th ed. (New York: McGraw Hill, 1962).

Guide to High-Performance Investing, By the Editors of Investor's Business Daily, (Los Angeles. CA: O'Neil Data Systems. Inc., 1993).

Hall, Alvin D., *Getting Started in Stocks,* (New York: Wiley, 1992).

Keys, Thomas and David Miller, *The Global Investor: How to Buy Stocks Around the World,* (Chicago, IL: Longman Financial Services Publishers, 1990).

Leeb, Stephen, Market Timing for the Nineties: The five key signals for when to buy, hold and sell, 1st ed. (New York: Harper Collins Publishers, 1993).

Little, Jeffrey and Lucien Rhodes, *Understanding Wall Street,* (Cockeysville, MD: Liberty Publishing Co., 1978).

Loll, Leo M. and Julian G. Buckley, *The Over-the-Counter Securities Markets,* 4th ed., (Englewood Cliffs, NJ: Prentice-Hall, 1981).

Lowe, Janet, *Keys to Investing in International Stocks,* (Hauppauge, NY: Barron's, 1992).

Malkiel, Burton G., *A Random Walk Down Wall Street,* 2nd college ed., (New York: Norton, 1981).

O'Neil, William J., How to Make Money in Stocks: A winning system in good times or bad, 2nd ed., (New York: McGraw-Hill, 1995).

Shaefer, Joseph L., Bringing Home the Gold: 10 Keys to Winning the Investment Decathlon, (Homewood, IL: Dow Jones-Irwin, 1989).

Shaw, Kathryn, *Investment Clubs: A Team Approach to the Stock Market,* (Chicago, IL: Dearborn Financial Publications, 1995).

Siegel, Jeremy J., *Stocks for the Long Run: A Guide to Selecting Markets for Long-Term Growth*, (Burr Ridge, IL: Irwin Professional Publishing, 1994).

Slatter, John, *Straight Talk About Stock Investing,* (New York: McGraw-Hill, 1995).

Stone, Dan G., How to Invest in the Market: The '90s Guide to Wall Street, (New York: Madison Pub. Associates, 1990).

Treasury Bills, Notes, and Bonds

Tucker, James F., *Buying Treasury Securities at Federal Reserve Banks,* (Richmond, VA: Federal Reserve Bank of Richmond, 1982).

Bartolini. Leonardo, *Treasury Bill Auctions: Issues And Uses.* (Washington, DC: International Monetary Fund, 1994). Series title: IMF working paper: WP/94/135.

Duffee, Gregory R., *Idiosyncratic Variation of Treasury Bill Yields,* (Washington, DC: Division of Research and Statistics, Division of Monetary Affairs, Federal Reserve Board, 1994). Series title: Finance and economics discussion series; 94-28.

Information About Marketable Treasury Securities (Bills, Notes And Bonds), Rev. 7/91, (Washington, DC: Dept. of the Treasury, Bureau of the Public Debt, 1991).

ABOUT THE AUTHOR

Roger Neal Smith has been involved in business and financial management and consulting for more than twenty-five years. He has had the rare opportunity of working on both sides of the investing area – as a stockbroker and money manager, as well as the Chairman of the Board and Chief Executive Officer of a publicly-traded company. As a result, he has been afforded the opportunity of viewing the world of finance from contrasting perspectives. In fact, since he and his CFO prepared the documents required to take a company public, he has personally interfaced with many of the U.S. securities regulatory agencies.

He currently serves as the Chief Executive Officer of Smith Food & Beverage Group, which develops, markets and distributes food and beverages internationally. Prior to his tenure at Smith Food & Beverage group, he founded and served as the President and CEO of OBN Holdings – an international entertainment, import/export and consulting company.

Mr. Smith's experience includes providing consulting services in the areas of finance, operations and marketing to both American and Japanese private enterprises, and to the United States federal government. Prior to starting OBN Holdings, Mr. Smith served as a Financial Consultant with Salomon Smith Barney, one of the world's largest securities firms. During that time, he was responsible for providing financial analysis, portfolio management, asset management, financial planning, investment advice, and product research services. During his tenure at the firm, Mr. Smith managed over $150 million in assets for more than 600 business and individual clients worldwide. Before working at Salomon Smith Barney, Mr. Smith was a Principal in The Creighton Group where he provided financial, strategic marketing, technology transfer and research services to both large and small businesses.

Since 1986, Mr. Smith has taught classes in business and ethics at various universities, including UCLA; California State University, Fullerton; California State University, Los Angeles; California State University, Northridge; California State University, Dominguez Hills; and Santa Monica College. Mr. Smith also served as the Chairman of the Board of Trustees for the Phillips Graduate Institute and was a member of the Board of Trustees for the California School of Professional Psychology.

Mr. Smith earned a Masters of Business degree from the University of Chicago and a Bachelor of Arts degree in photography and design from the University of Illinois, Chicago. He is able to speak, read and write Japanese.